Reasonably Believable Things

Robert Watson

Copyright © 2022 by Robert Watson.

All rights reserved. No part of this document may be reproduced or transmitted in any form without prior written permission of the publisher.

ISBN: 978-1-7375622-0-7 (softcover)
ISBN: 978-1-7375622-1-7 (Nook/ePub)
ISBN: 978-1-7375622-2-7 (Kindle)

Library of Congress subject headings:
    Creationism.
    Bible and evolution.

BISAC Subject Headings
    RELIGION / Christian Theology / Apologetics
    RELIGION / Religion & Science
    RELIGION / Christian Living / Social Issues
    RELIGION / Biblical Studies / Prophecy

All scripture references are taken from the King James Version (KJV).

Contents

Contents		ii
Preface		v
	My Experience	ix
	Why I Am Writing	xv
Introduction		**xix**
	What If?	xix
	Organization of the Book	xxii
1	**Scoffers**	**1**
	Since the Fathers Fell Asleep	3
	Willingly Ignorant	6
	Walking After Their Own Lusts	12
	Overflowed with Water	14
	What Is a Scoffer?	18
	Why This Prophecy?	19
2	**What Can We Know?**	**23**
	Objective Reality	26
	Irrefutable Truth	29
	Knowledge and Reasoning	31

Contents   iii

    I Think Therefore I Am   36
    Logical Reasoning   43
    Incompleteness   48
    What Can We Learn?   51
    Proof in the Natural Sciences   54
    Occam's Razor   59
    Faith is Universal   63
    Conclusion   64

3 What Can We Believe?   **67**
    Limited Utility of Proof   67
    Something More   70
    Skeptics   73
    The Search   74
    The Evaluation   82
    Prophecies   88

4 Perilous Times   **93**
    Having a Form of Godliness   94
    Lovers of Their Own Selves   96
    Despisers of Those That Are Good   97
    The Days of Noah   98
    What Should We Do?   101
    Knowledge   112
    Summary   114

5 Christians   **115**

6 Suggested Reading   **125**

Preface

I address this book to that segment of Christianity that believes in God as our literal and specific creator, the one who authored the universe and carefully directed the inscription and compilation of the Bible as His communication to us. This segment of Christianity has many critics. Some critics are quiet, some are outspoken, some have little knowledge, and some are highly educated and articulate. It's not unusual for these critics to insist that a belief in God, especially a belief that the events described in Bible are literally true, cannot be rationally maintained in the light of what mankind now knows.

Their premise, whether implied or explicitly stated, is that the science of evolution has dispensed with the need for a creator. Any belief in a creator can (allegedly) no longer be justified. This premise seems to have developed through a series of progressions.

Initially, science was interested in the study of the processes at work within creation. For Christians, it is the study of these natural processes that God created for the routine operation of the universe. This is certainly reasonable. We can always explain natural processes by saying that God "did that," we just don't know how.

Actually, there are many things in creation that are quite real, but we don't know how they were done. But such an explanation does nothing to help us to understand just what it is that God created, which is the real goal of scientific study. So, the initial premise in science was to understand the parts of creation that were defined by a fixed set of rules or laws. It is that part of creation that we are able understand, even though God did not explain it in His written Word.

Scientists, who in their personal views don't want to consider a creator, alter this initial premise by saying that God has no place in science. That is their view, but it isn't shared by many of the foundational figures in the history of modern science.

Over time, the number and influence of non-Christian scientists has grown, and the view has shifted to one that holds that the discoveries of science are in conflict with a creation by God. Actually, it is the scientist that is in conflict, as the last chapter of science has yet to be written. This influence has caused some "apparent Christians" to abandon their faith and embrace apostasy. Still, some Christians have decided that they must adapt the Word of God to fit these scientific discoveries to mitigate the conflict. Today, we have a spectrum of adaptations that range from mild, seemingly harmless ideas, to a brutal disregard of God's Word that leaves no room for a literal creator. The next step in the progression brings us to where we are today. A premise that denies even the possibility of a creator.

Our critics may shy away from saying that the impossibility of a creator as described in the Bible has been irrefutably proven. They know that such proof is far from existing. But when we are told that belief in a creator cannot be rationally supported to the extent that such belief is intolerable, they imply that such proof *does* exist.

For me, this has always been the cutting edge of the atheist argument. Does such proof exist? If not, how soon before it does exist? I consider the question important because if there is no possibility that the critics are wrong, or if they can convince Christians that they are not wrong, then Christians are, of all men, most pitiful (I Corinthians 15:16–19).

In present-day culture, many Christians have accepted that the critics are not wrong. They may believe they are holding on to a faith in God contrary to reason. I find this reaction infuriating. Christians do not need to think that they must set aside reason to maintain their belief and faith. It isn't sufficient to just say that Christianity is reasonable. There must be support for such a claim. I suggest that said reason be approached from two directions—that such critics are not necessarily right, and that we can show that belief in the literal God as described in the Bible is reasonable.

Some readers who are familiar with these issues may object on the grounds that belief in what is written in the Bible is much more than just reasonable; in fact, the evidence is overwhelming. I choose to proceed on the basis that it is "merely reasonable" because, as will be discussed, belief does not precede faith. No one will be able to recognize the countless evidences for a universe created by God just as God has described it unless they first have faith to believe it is *possible*.

The critic does not believe that creation by God is possible. This precludes faith, the essential precursor for belief. The critics' beliefs are then in accord with their faith and they become blind to any form of contrary evidence.

The acquisition of knowledge is a lifelong process where small faith paves the way for small belief, which in turn enables stronger faith and stronger belief. No one is exempt from this sequence, critic or Christian. Both are the product of their faith. So, in this book, we will together discover reasons why Christians can know with greater certainty than any other fact the human race can establish, that our critics can be wrong. My intention is to open the door for others so that they can see that Christianity is not just pointless faith, it is a faith leading to a belief that can be held on rational grounds. No discovery has been made that can refute that.

My Experience

Like many in my generation, I grew up in a Christian household where I was taught Christian beliefs. I also grew up in a culture and educational system that frequently disagreed with those beliefs. At times, this conflict can seem so subtle as to be almost subliminal in its influence. At other times, it's obvious that we are being told that we must put aside our ignorance and embrace new beliefs—beliefs that are incompatible with what we have been taught. This influence is quite powerful, and it is all too common to see young students who were well-taught as children discard what they once believed true and embrace these "new" ideas.

The influence of our culture can be powerful, even for those who are not persuaded to discard what our predecessors have taught. An example I find is a not quite conscious feeling that the Word of God is fragile. That we must be very careful with it because it is not able to withstand direct contact with advanced human knowledge and wisdom. We don't explicitly think of the Word of God this way, but we behave as if we do.

If we have any excuse for such weakness, it is a feeling that we are not adequate to defend the Word of God against those who claim it is all a fraud. Perhaps this feeling is legitimate, but our error is in thinking that defending God's Word depends on our skill. The feeling that God's plans will fail if we fail. There is no need to worry—God's intention is to engage us in His plans and then to succeed, even if we fail. We probably all know someone who acts as if they are the only force keeping God's plans on track. They will someday discover that God is even able to overcome their "help" and accomplish everything He intends.

My Experience

We may also feel that if we try to defend God's Word and fail, our faith fails also. This is a much more unpleasant feeling. We all know that God will be OK. Ourselves? Not so much. There are apostate Christians who are quite vocal about how they became apostate when they realized that science or philosophy had discredited the Word of God. So, we avoid comparing God's Word to human knowledge, just to be safe.

Is it OK to just avoid the problem, stick our heads in the sand so-to-speak? Perhaps. You may be familiar with the quotation of Pericles, "Just because you do not take an interest in politics doesn't mean politics won't take an interest in you." Similarly, you may not be interested in God's critics, but they are interested in you. As history progresses, it becomes increasingly difficult to be neutral. You may need to know that God's Word is quite sturdy and will not fail us. We may fail God. We will fail God if we do nothing with the faith that has been given to us.

The rules of this conflict are not fair—a creator cannot lose. God's critics can appear reasonable when they have the home-court advantage, which science has emerged as. It is a place where the validity of human knowledge and the error of God's knowledge is assumed from the beginning. It is a place where the Word of God appears to be foolish (I Corinthians 2:14), and that is by design. The Father's power, the Holy Spirit's wisdom, and the Son's sacrifice cannot be stopped. We can't just sit on the bench and watch God go—God insists that we participate.

As a student, like most of us have been, I felt and understood the critic's influence. Probably with the help of an inborn stubbornness, I wanted some plausible justification before accepting each new idea. Even so, I began to discover that I had accepted many such plausible ideas that later proved to be quite questionable. When I became a teacher, and older, I gained a greater appreciation for how little our students are able to defend themselves when a respected teacher presents facts with an astounding degree of bias.

Throughout higher education, there is an emphasis on what is called "critical reasoning." Critical reasoning is the process of evaluating the things we are told to determine if they are true or not. It is a good goal, and probably one of the most important things we could teach students. Some students have difficulty achieving this skill, while to others, it seems like an obvious procedure.

Our first application of critical reasoning should be to evaluate the person who is teaching it. Professors are

My Experience

not immune to the faults they are trying to teach students to avoid, specifically bias and fallacy. In fact, in my view, they are much worse than average. There is something about an advanced education that causes us to believe we have acquired immunity to these faults. Our critical reasoning should be telling us that is not likely.

In practice, when we teach, we always and unavoidably end by teaching what we (the professor) believe—beliefs fully loaded with all of the professors' bias and even some fallacy. We have no choice. If we don't teach what we believe, we have nothing to teach. We do well to minimize our bias to the extent that we are able. If we think we teach without bias, it is because we (erroneously) believe we have no bias. I am especially skeptical of that kind of conceit.

The student who has genuinely learned to think critically can identify these faults. Those who don't have the potential to be worse for their education. Some students will become teachers themselves, adding their own bias and fallacies to those they were taught. In turn, this is what is imparted to the next generation of students. Again, we do our students a great disservice if we are not diligent to identify and remove as much of our own bias as possible.

I personally think good critical reasoning skills require a person to have a healthy balance of stubbornness and open-mindedness. With too much obstinacy, you are not able to learn new things that are valid. If too agreeable, a person will accept new things they should have known were invalid. I have plenty of stubbornness, but I seem to have learned, relearned, and unlearned a few things. I like to think I have passable critical reasoning skills, but that may be a prejudicial assessment. Actually, my critical reasoning tells me I am biased and must identify potential bias so that I can examine it closely.

I have always enjoyed science and it has been a significant part of my education. In my earlier years, I had to reconcile the things I believed and the new things I was learning. I have invested much of my time examining (and re-examining) the conflicts I found.

Frequently, these conflicting beliefs revolve around something that is written in the Bible that can't be literally true. Something that just couldn't have happened the way it is written ... could it? We explain away what is written so that it seems plausible even to someone who does not believe in God. As we do this, we diminish our own faith and possibly the faith of those around us. It ignores a very simple question—if we believe that we and everything else were created by God, why would He provide us with erroneous information?

Friends have, at times, brought to my attention plausible reason to believe that what is written could and did happen just as it is recorded. It is embarrassing to have to accept that my faith was too weak to believe something that is now shown to be believable. Eventually, I grew tired of being embarrassed by my disbelief in reasonably believable things.

Must the critics be right? This question has challenged me all of my life and consumed countless hours of contemplation. If the answer is yes, I too must discard everything I once believed and embrace new and incompatible beliefs. But if the answer is no, then comes the hard part. How do I know? How sure can I be?

Why I Am Writing

After many years, many experiences, lessons learned and observed, I feel blessed to have reached an understanding that I am comfortable with. When some belief that I hold to be very important is challenged, I must still reexamine why I have that belief. Not so that I can respond to the challenger, that is a skill I never had. But rather, to respond to my own need for understanding. My own need to assure myself that my bias has been satisfactorily accounted for. That the challenger is not presenting a new argument that I had not previously considered. Or if it is a new argument, that it doesn't change what I already know. And if it does change what I already know, make the necessary adjustments.

When I look back over this journey and at younger generations, I realize that perhaps I can be of some help. That is the impetus for writing this book. All of what is written here I have collected for my own personal use, to understand the world around me, to understand my place in it, to understand myself, what I believe and why I believe it.

God has always been quite generous with me–I have always known that. Perhaps His generosity has been so that I might share what I have learned with others. Others who believe the gospel, the good news that God has provided someone, Jesus, the only begotten son of God, who is equal to God, and who took upon himself the punishment for the sins I have committed. These are the people who are facing the same conflict of beliefs that I have faced and need the same answers. God has given me so many opportunities to learn, from pastors, parents, educators, and generally the world around me. Those who do not (yet) have the gospel will not likely benefit from what I have written here, and it will not likely change their minds. So, I don't present this as a primarily evangelistic-work. I commend this book to the reader for the purpose of strengthening their faith in a God who has shown consistent faithfulness toward a world in which He has many opponents.

Must our critics be right? No, they can be wrong—they can be very wrong. Read on to learn why you can believe that.

Introduction

Must our critics be right? The question is always valid, but the answer depends on who is asking and when. I will be considering the critics of Jesus' second coming from a western perspective, and at a time when many contend that humanity has (or should have) outgrown this fundamental belief. I contend that we are well-prepared to answer this question because God has not left us to fend for ourselves. He has provided the information we need to respond in turn.

What If?

What if our critics are right? What is the significance of that scenario? The human race left to its own devices is the highest authority in the known universe. What is that like? I think we have a taste of that already.

As long ago as the Renaissance, secular intellectualism asserted the belief that the human condition could be better served by the pursuit of ideals and goals that are distinct from previous times. Those times were dominated by religious constraint. Humanity began to take a more active and deliberate role in choosing its own future, promising to obtain a better one than the church had provided. While the church could promise forgiveness, perfection, and eternal life "someday", humans promised these things immediately.

The ideas of secular intellectualism continued to build through subsequent milestones of cultural and intellectual development, including Enlightenment and Modernism, until at its zenith, it appeared that utopia was within reach. The promises and constraints that religion had provided would no longer be needed. There seemed to be no limit to what men could achieve. Utopia would be the crowning achievement and validation of the humanist initiative.

Today, the institutions that were to guide us to this bright and prosperous future have themselves provided definitive limits to what humans can achieve. Knowledge and reason have bounds that we do not appear to be able to overcome. As human achievement increased, so have the problems we were supposed to defeat: savagery, death, suffering, and injustice. Rather than achieve higher levels of peace, we have discovered more death than the human race has ever known. We have learned to heal and also to kill with a speed and efficiency that would have astounded our ancestors. While we have cured disease, previously unknown and increasingly ominous diseases now loom on the horizon. Living conditions are better for everyone, including those living in poverty, than at any time in the past, yet arguably we are less content than ever before. The great projects to build utopian societies have provided poverty, oppression, and death on a scale never before seen on the earth. Humanism has suffered tragedy as much as triumph.

In the wake of these failures, and with the promise of unlimited human potential now tarnished, the human race has begun to be disillusioned with modernism, the most recent and most ambitious product of humanism. It is at this point in history that we now find ourselves. For better or worse, we live in interesting times.

I see little or no indication that disappointment in modernism is triggering a reversion to a former manner of living, at least not in a deliberate way. Changes that seemingly must come are only now emerging and are evidenced by such things as postmodernism, philosophy's self-immolation. Before we join this rather extreme reaction, perhaps we should ask, what went wrong? How did our birthright of peace, harmony, and prosperity turn into hopelessness and despair? Because if we dig deep enough, most of the social projects of today are little more than activities that help us to avoid dwelling on the inevitable conclusions the modernist thinker must now reach. Humanism has failed us.

We could spend a lifetime pondering this state of affairs and trying to come to grips with it. There are many who do just that. They try to understand the world in a way that will restore some peace of mind. I don't see anyone having much success with that. They feel that if they push a meaningful agenda or join a righteous movement, then they can be "part of the solution" even though the problem never gets better.

"Someday" continues to get closer while utopia moves further way. What if our critics are right? I think the critics would do well to re-examine their own beliefs.

Organization of the Book

If God created this world, it seems reasonable to see what He has to say about our critics. I believe that He has indeed had something to say, and in doing so,

Organization of the Book

has assured us that His plans that were established before the world was, are on schedule. Even better, He has also told us what we can expect for our future and that this future is quite secure.

This book begins with an examination of the apostle Peter's prophecy recorded in the third chapter of Peter's second epistle. Here, I assert that this prophecy is now being fulfilled and that fulfillment is essentially complete. In doing so, I identify the focus of the prophecy (scoffers) as a group of persons that are opposed to God and who use science to discredit Him.

Scoffers claim that science enables them to dispense with a creator and to rationally dismiss anyone who does not agree. Science is an integral part of our culture at this time and most of us place a great deal of confidence in whatever "science" has to say. However, science is not a person with a voice, it is a collection of disciplines in which we find practitioners—scientists. Unfortunately, these practitioners are subject to the usual assortment of human faults, which include engaging in exaggeration, hyperbole, and repetition of things they have heard but have no direct knowledge. There would be less harm done if these faults did not occur in the context of "expert opinion". Persons outside of science may, and based on my own life experience do, have an unwarranted confidence in the infallibility of science. This is the focus of Chapter 2, where I explore the idea of knowledge—where do we get it and how reliable is it. My intention is to show that the knowledge we produce is much less reliable than we generally believe, less reliable than scientists themselves often believe.

Science has provided us with excellent tools for the purpose of acquiring knowledge, but without examining the origin of the knowledge we don't know how useful or harmful that knowledge might be. At the conclusion of Chapter 2, we may have the impression that the pursuit of knowledge is futile. I do not want to leave the reader in such a pessimistic frame of mind. Chapter 3 considers the prospect of finding knowledge that is possibly more reliable than Chapter 2 suggests, or at least the most reliable knowledge available to us.

Chapter 3 provides a compelling case for a creator God, just as the Bible describes. I think it inescapable that there will be those who are not quite convinced. What more can we do? No one will believe anything that they do not have the faith to believe. In Chapter 4 , doubtful readers will be given something to think about. Until now, we have made arguments based on what has already occurred. Things prophesied in advance, but already behind us. For some, that dimin-

Organization of the Book

ishes its value as evidence, maybe because it is too familiar.

Chapter 4 discusses the next development for humanity. In this chapter, I examine the prophecy recorded by the apostle Paul in the third chapter of the second book of Timothy. We can't say precisely when this prophecy will occur, but I think it to be soon. If we see the things described in this prophecy come to pass, they will be in stark contrast to the future that has been described by our critics. That contrast should make it increasingly evident that the critics have it wrong and the Bible, with the prophecy God has provided there, is correct. Perhaps this will provide just enough additional evidence (it will become evidence after it has happened) to help remove the doubts of a few more people.

In Chapter 5, I try to provide some perspective for Christians living in the present and near future. There may be readers who were not already familiar with what I have written and who may get a feeling of disorientation. I hope that this chapter will help by placing the things written in this book into a Christian context.

Chapter 6 is a list of suggested readings on some of the topics that are touched on. This list is focused on sources that may not be familiar to the reader. Perhaps I can provide a platform that makes these additional and very informative resources more accessible.

The apostle Peter wrote: *Your adversary the devil, as a roaring lion, walketh about, seeking whom he may devour...* (Peter 5:8, KJV)

I trust this book will provide the reader with a measure of defense against these attacks on the faith of those who live in these interesting times.

1. Scoffers

...there shall come in the last days scoffers, walking after their own lusts, And saying, Where is the promise of his coming? for since the fathers fell asleep, all things continue as they were from the beginning of the creation. For this they willingly are ignorant of, that by the word of God the heavens were of old, and the earth standing out of the water and in the water: Whereby the world that then was, being overflowed with water, perished: But the heavens and the earth, which are now, by the same word are kept in store, reserved unto fire against the day of judgment and perdition of ungodly men.
2 Peter 3:3–7

There are many prophecies identified as last days or latter days, and often without additional detail about when those days will be. Such prophecies do not all refer to the same period of time—often, they don't. The lack of such information that would allow us to project when these days will appear suggests that those who live before the prophecy is fulfilled don't need to know exactly when they will occur. We just know that such events will happen. Those who do

Scoffers

see these prophecies come to pass will be able to recognize them, and thereby gain an understanding of the events happening around themselves, where they live in God's timeline, and what they will need to do in response to those events.

Through much or all of the 20th century, there have been people who recognized that Peter's prophecy was being fulfilled. Looking back, we can see that fulfillment began even earlier. Now I think we are seeing the fulfillment of this prophecy come to an end. From our present vantage point, we should be able to assemble a clear picture of how this prophecy has been realized, and that should help us to understand ourselves, our culture, and our future. Even more importantly, we can be encouraged by a vivid example of God watching over His creation.

This prophecy describes a group of people that God characterized as scoffers. We are told what they do and how they do it. This should help us to determine if indeed we are living in the times that are described here. We are also told why they do what they do. That is particularly interesting since it is very hard for us to attribute motives to other people's actions in more than a speculative manner. Yet, more interesting is that God tells us how to know that these scoffers are in error and how to address their error.

When we have finished with this prophecy, I hope you will be able to see that these opponents of God have constructed an elaborate argument to discredit God, to undermine the faith of the faithful, and to place a stumbling stone in the path of those who would consider the call of their Savior.

Since the Fathers Fell Asleep

There is an idea in geology known as uniformitarianism that captures the proposition that the physical processes we see today have been ongoing in the past such that those processes are responsible for the geologic features we now observe. This term, from the 19th century, was developed as an alternative to catastrophism (i.e. the flood) to explain the geologic development of the earth.

The idea of uniformitarianism has since been utilized in other branches of science as a means of describing a past that cannot be observed. This is an important point to bear in mind. We can only observe the present. We cannot observe, experiment on, or repeat the past. So, while an idea such as uniformitarianism may be useful or interesting as a possible guide to what has happened in the past, we should never make the mistake of over-estimating its quality as evidence. As evidence for or against any theory, present observation is always superior to an extrapolation into the past.

Perhaps with some modification to account for observations that undeniably do not fit the uniformitarian model, the idea is very widely accepted today. So much so that there is widespread agreement that the issue is now decided and no further debate is warranted. Uniformitarianism provides the accepted account of the development of the earth, and now, the universe itself. Catastrophism is discarded as an erroneous belief once held by our unlearned ancestors and a few stubborn and weak-minded fools today.

Uniformitarianism directly contradicts the record found in the book of Genesis and presents believers with a serious dilemma. Why did God not tell us that the earth was very old, that He spent many ages slowly developing it, rather than speaking it into existence in six days? Why would he do that? He has to know that such a false account of creation will give believers a legitimate reason to doubt the rest of what He has said. Many sincere believers face the necessity of accepting scientific fact while also holding to their faith that God is trustworthy and faithful. Some have invented ways to reconcile scripture with the historical timeline implied by uniformitarianism.

Others, being weaker in faith, have to some degree, either consciously or subconsciously, accepted that God is a little less honest with us than we might have hoped that He would be.

This is prime among the purposes for which God gave us II Peter 3. He knew this conflict would come and demonstrated His complete control over the history of the earth in the most powerful and convincing way—by telling us about the present, 2,000 years before it happened. In these verses, He told us in advance that scoffers would appear. The identity of the scoffers is verified by the words ... *for since the fathers fell asleep, all things continue as they were from the beginning of the creation.* This is a concise description of uniformitarianism written 1,800 years before the theory was proposed.

This prophecy is encouraging to those who are discouraged by scoffers. And for those discouraged by the scoffer's overwhelming success in purging the knowledge of God from our culture, He adds this additional word of encouragement: The scoffer will not be with us forever. The earth will once again be destroyed, but not before every effort has been made to save everyone who is willing to believe what He has written.

God wrote that He created the universe and destroyed the earth in a flood. Scoffers have come and told us that they can prove otherwise. How does God respond? He doubled down on the creation and flood accounts of Genesis. And God is saying that we should be more impressed by the fulfillment of a 2,000-year-old prophecy than speculation about a history that had no witnesses.

Willingly Ignorant

Scoffers are willingly ignorant of the fact that the earth was created by the word of God and destroyed in a flood. How are they *willingly* ignorant? In Peter's day, it could be said that people were willingly ignorant since Genesis was extant and many knew what was written there. But these scoffers were future to the prophet and they are willingly ignorant in a way their predecessors were not.

What would make scoffers ignorant in a way previous generations were not? One possibility is in the study of geology. Prior to the development and widespread knowledge of geology, the only understanding we have of creation and the flood would have come from the book of Genesis. Today, there is at least some knowledge of geology throughout our society. Even without a formal education on the subject, there is a common knowledge of the history of the earth, big-bang, evolution, dinosaurs, impacts from meteors, etc.

A sustained and detailed study of geology should produce evidence of the flood, or a lack thereof. Scoffers say the evidence does not exist, God says it does, and believers must decide. One group of believers says, "If God said it, that settles it." God bless them, but that doesn't help when they are asked (sincerely) why God's Word doesn't agree with the evidence. Why God didn't just tell us the truth to begin with. Another group says in effect, "A million scoffers can't be wrong." I've been there—you just can't argue with what "everyone" knows to be true. Sometimes, what everyone knows to be true is wrong. "Everyone" has been wrong before, and "everyone" will be wrong again.

If blind confidence in one belief or the other is not satisfactory, what should we do? Peter's prophecy tells us the evidence is there, all we need to do is look for it. And that is pretty easy since geologists have done the leg-work for us. Their observations are good—it is some of their conclusions God takes issue with. We can review the evidence they have collected, and their conclusions too, and then draw our own conclusions. We are free to accept the generally accepted conclusions or make our own. This, after all, is what scientists are supposed to do. And do not be intimidated into thinking that "non-scientists" have no business engaging in this discussion. In science, there is no vetting of credentials before ideas can be presented. It is the ideas themselves that matter regardless of their origin. A "scientist" is a person who engages in this activity on a consistent basis. Such a person will obtain knowledge to support their activity, either formally or informally. Everyone, scientists and non-scientists, should be using what reasoning skills they have to validate all of the information presented to them. Many will do the job badly, scientists and non-scientists alike.

How do you avoid ignorance by evaluating scientific knowledge for yourself when you aren't a scientist? It really isn't that difficult in the context of the world in our immediate vicinity. When someone makes a claim about life on Mars, we would need a great deal of study in several areas of specialization in order to know if the claims were well-founded or not. It is much easier to evaluate claims about the world that is immediately in front of us, and that should make geology of special interest to us. We are literally walking on geology every day. This will be more difficult if the geology that is immediately in front of you is covered in concrete and asphalt. Fortunately, that was not true for me. I grew up confronted by many things that seemed contradictory to the facts I learned in school. But "a million scientists can't be wrong", so I concluded that I must be wrong.

It is said that uniformitarianism has displaced catastrophism and the issue is closed. While that does describe the current state of science as it is commonly practiced, it does not mean that there are no scientists that question uniformitarianism today. Such scientists do exist and their work is available to us. These are people who have taken the same evidences that are used to support popular beliefs about the origins of the earth and show that additional theories are also supported. These scientists have a variety of perspectives. Some consider a creator without being specific about who the creator is. Others identify the creator as the literal God described in Genesis, including a literal account of creation. All of these views share a rogue status in the scientific community. I will refer to them collectively as dissenting scientists.

For the believer trying to understand the discrepancy between what scoffers are saying and what God has said, there are two aspects of dissent that interest us. First, these scientists catalog the evidence that dis-

Scoffers

agrees with more popular theories. In my own life, I could personally observe simple things that didn't seem to support the scoffers. Scientists who specialize in the relevant fields have a much longer list that contains more serious issues that scoffers don't seem to be able to explain. These issues are important because they give us insight into the quality of the various theories. The scientist who considers only the evidence that supports a theory and disregards or minimizes contradictory evidence places himself in a poor position to arrive at the truth.

The other aspect of dissenting science that we want to consider are theories that explain the same evidence scoffers use, yet arrive at a different conclusion. In particular, conclusions that are to some degree consistent with what God has written. Don't make the false assumption that these scientists are believers; some are and some are not. They may just be scientists who are less prone to willful ignorance. What we want to know of their theories is this: How well do they explain the evidence?

It is not my purpose to get into the specifics of the various theories and evidence. There are many books and other publications on these subjects written for a variety of audiences. I would not be able to do justice to the subject in this space. Fortunately, the internet has made this information readily available, and I list a few resources in the last chapter.

Do we dare to consider what such dissident scientists say? They might be crackpots, after all. I would not suggest that we accept their theories without critical evaluation any more than I suggest we should do so with the claims of scoffers. If we are to be rational, we give all competing ideas the same degree of critical rigor and lean in the direction of those that best match our observations. No scientific study explains all of our observations completely. If one did, there would no longer be a need for additional exploration.

What we need to do is measure the quality of each theory by the degree to which it conforms to the observations we have made instead of the size of its fan base. The quality of a scientist is measured by the quality of his work, but the quality a work is not measured by the quality of the scientist. I propose that you evaluate competing theories for yourself, be equally critical in your evaluation of each, and draw your own conclusions. Each individual will have to bear the consequences of their conclusions and beliefs.

Scoffers

Walking After Their Own Lusts

Why would scoffers be willingly ignorant? Because they are walking after their own lusts. Notice that the verse does not say "walking in lusts," it says *their own* lusts. This is a small distinction to make, but I think it is important. How would their own lusts differ from lusts in general? Like the description of uniformitarianism, I think this is an elegant depiction of humanism, written many years before that system of thought rose to its current prominence.

We expect a person's behavior to reflect their character and beliefs. We expect Christians to behave in a manner that reflects their belief in God, which includes God's instructions regarding the manner in which Christians are to conduct themselves. When a society has a large population of believers, the influence that these Christians have is reflected in the laws and norms of that society. Scoffers are opposed to having these laws and norms imposed on everyone who lives in such a society. In addition, scoffers who go against these common values will face constant reminders by the culture around them that they fall short of their creator's standards.

A creator necessarily has authority over his creation and a creation has an intrinsic obligation to its creator. Scoffers do not want to acknowledge their obligation to their creator because they want to walk after their own lusts instead. Unbelievers have often stated that they have and should have the freedom to disregard the demands and expectations of a God they do not recognize. Scoffers go a step further.

Scoffers react by striving to dismantle the laws and norms that conflict with their own desires. A variety of strategies can be seen to be active in our society, but the one Peter refers to are the efforts to discredit God. By casting doubt on Jesus' return, they cast doubt on his resurrection, which casts doubt on the veracity of God's Word to us. This, in turn, casts doubt on the quality of God's people whose influence is offensive to scoffers. If God's people can be marginalized in this way, the influence of their values can be diminished. Laws and norms can be changed and scoffers will be freer to pursue their own lusts. To the scoffer, this is what it means to be free.

Let us not make the mistake of sympathizing with the scoffers' claim that they have a right to a life that is free from God. Such a right should not supersede the right of a Christian to live in a manner that is consistent with what God has written and to express their beliefs.

Overflowed with Water

Scoffers are ignorant of the fact that the earth that was created by God's word was destroyed in a flood. It has been pointed out by others that if this flood were regional, Noah could have walked to a place outside the flood zone much faster and easier than building a boat and loading it with animals. The flood, according to God, was global. A flood of that extent just a few thousand years ago must leave a lot of evidence. It did.

Is this really important? Why not just avoid the flood issue and stick to evangelism or another Christian pursuit? Evangelism is impeded by the apparent credibility gap presented by scoffers. If we are to present a credible case for salvation, we will need to address all accusations raised by scoffers.

There are many who have taken up the task of addressing the erroneous claims of scoffers. Fittingly for our time are those that address the claim that science refutes creation. These people work in many different fields, such as biology, paleontology, and physics. Our prophecy addresses only geology and, indirectly, paleontology. I don't think that is an accident. When engaging scoffers on subjects such as evolutionary biology, much can be said in favor of creation. However, such apologists are handicapped by the presumption of a very old earth. If the earth is extremely old the popular scientific explanations appear reasonable and the scriptural account just plain wrong. If God's description of creation is correct, the narrative presented by scoffers is a house of cards, not supported by the observable evidence at all. If we are to address the scoffer's narrative, we can push on the top card (i.e., evolutionary biology) with some success, or go directly to the bottom card, bringing down the whole house.[1]

What is the bottom card? An earth of extreme old age.

Peter's prophecy says that the creation and global flood accounts in Genesis can explain our geologic observations and many scientists have provided plausible theories accordingly. So, what is the evidence that the earth is extremely old? The geologic column itself is not much of a guide. Instead, fossils and radiometric dating are used.

Geologic formations are dated by the fossils (index fossils) that are found in them. How is the age of the fossils known? Evolution is first assumed, and then the order in which the fossilized organisms evolved

---

[1] Note that the goal here is to set believer's minds at ease, not to persuade scoffers.

is estimated. The time needed for each evolutionary development is then estimated to produce a chronology for their development. As is widely known, the derivation of evolutionary lineages from the fossil record is complicated by, among other things, the so-called missing links. They are the shortage of fossils indicating transitions between highly dissimilar animals. This hampers the construction of a comprehensive order of evolution among these kinds of life.

The fossil record has another, and I think, greater problem in that it contains a large discontinuity known as the Cambrian explosion. This term describes the observation that the bulk of the fossil record begins in the Cambrian era. Something like 90% of evolutionary history is supposed to occur in strata that predate the Cambrian, yet those strata do not contain fossils usable for evolutionary reconstruction. If these evolutionary developments did not occur prior to the Cambrian era, then this very large part of evolutionary history occurred during the 25 million-year Cambrian era itself. There seems to be little explanation for why the organisms that are expected to appear in older strata left few or no fossils. Consequently, dating strata using index fossils becomes increasingly dubious beyond the most recent 10% of earth's history.

Radioactive isotopes are also used to determine the age of geologic features. Is that definitive? Apparently not. The theory on which radiometric dating is based seems very good. A great deal of effort has gone into the development and refinement of these techniques. The last step in vetting any scientific methodology is to compare experimental and theoretical results. A number of shortcomings have been found that limit confidence in the method. These shortcomings include repeatability (the ability to take multiple measurements of the sample or in the same strata with the same results) and consistency among different radiometric methods. While the theory of radiometric dating seems sound, experimental results leave much room to question their reliability.

What we should keep in mind is that the evidence for an old earth is far from conclusive. Several of the books listed in Chapter 6 discuss in detail the reasons we can believe that this is so. And if the earth is young, a recent global flood could provide an explanation for our observations of geology and paleontology that is at least as complete as those produced from the uniformitarian perspective. The apostle Peter is saying that the quality of the catastrophic (flood) theory is so good that scoffers must make an effort to avoid acknowledging it. Unless the earth is very old, the rest of the scoffer's house of cards collapses. It is for this reason uniformitarianism was given as the defining attribute of scoffers. A very old earth is necessary to give the rest of their claims the appearance of plausibility.

What Is a Scoffer?

So, what identifies a scoffer? Several criteria are provided and many people may satisfy one or more of them. But a scoffer should satisfy most, if not, all of these criteria. The first is very important: Scoffers ridicule the return (the second coming) of Jesus. The apostle Paul tells us that there is a special crown that God will award to all those who love His appearing (return) (II Timothy 4). These are clearly not scoffers.

The next criterion is that scoffers adopt is a theory of origins specifically dismissing the account provided by God in the book of Genesis. Many, including many Christians, meet this criterion. But as previously stated, this criterion alone does not identify a person as a scoffer. Scoffers also hold to their belief in a theory of origins despite clear evidence showing their theories to be wrong.

The third criterion is that scoffers will place their faith in theories they should know are wrong because they don't want to hear that God disapproves of the lusts they indulge in. They don't want to hear that God is calling them to put those lusts away to grow into something better.

Why This Prophecy?

It is well-said that God does not give us prophecy to make us prophets. There are numerous reasons prophecy is given and several of them are present here. If we read the remainder of the chapter quoted above, we see that there was an immediate application of this prophecy. It provided encouragement to the early believers who may have been discouraged when Christ's return did not take place as soon as they had thought it would. Certainly, those early believers were facing scoffers who ridiculed the foolishness of believing in the resurrection and return of Jesus. When His return didn't happen soon, the scoffers appeared to be correct.

This prophecy is an especially valuable source of encouragement and support to today's believers, who must bear the burden of scoffing. Scoffers are active in discouraging believers, telling them that science

Scoffers

has proven that their belief is in vain and that only the weak-minded need God as a crutch by which to cope with life. God provides this prophecy to counter their arguments by telling us about scoffers 2,000 years before they appear. Note the contrast: Scoffers are telling us of a distant-past with no witnesses while God is telling us of a future we can now observe for ourselves.

In addition to encouragement, this prophecy provides instruction for responding to scoffers. You may or may not have a need to respond to scoffers in person, but every believer living today has a personal need to respond to the scoffer's accusations. Accusations that God has lied, that there is no resurrection, and that our belief is in vain. Even if you are secure in your faith, other believers may not be. God provides prophecy so that you can encourage them. And then there are the lost, who hear the words of scoffers and feel they have no choice but to accept their bold claims of authority as truth. In an era when scoffers appear to hold a winning hand, how do we respond? Can we respond?

A consistent theme in scripture is a call to reason. To obtain knowledge and wisdom and apply them in our lives. This is a prominent theme in the books of Proverbs and Ecclesiastes. Something all created living things have in common, from animals to angels, is a capacity to learn.

Science done well is a meticulous application of reason for the purpose of increasing our understanding of the universe in which we find ourselves. The universe has clearly yielded to rational study and it seems that God has intended it this way. Scripture is continually calling people to draw informed conclusions from facts presented and this prophecy is no exception. It doesn't simply make a statement *believers good, scoffers bad.* It points to where we can find evidence to support the statements being made about scoffers. A rational inquiry is called for.

Consider this: In the Scripture, if God's communication to us is not reliable, then God is not reliable either. If God lies or misleads us in His Word, obeying His commands is pointless. We might argue that a creator that can construct the universe, the earth, and everything living has no need to lie. And if God lies to us, then He isn't God and the scoffers are correct.

As the apostle Paul put it, if there is no resurrection (as God has told us there is), then we of all men are most miserable (I Corinthians 15:19). Either God has been truthful with us or our faith in Him is in vain. We

Scoffers

are told in this prophecy that the scoffers are wrong about creation and the flood. If we discover that the scoffers are correct, we have no reason to think the other things written in the Bible are true.

There are those who attempt, with varying degrees of success, to prove creation and the existence of a creator. God bless them, I enjoy reading what they have to say. I will not attempt to do so here because for our purposes that is putting the cart before the horse. I am convinced, and I will proceed on this basis, that proof of any assertion is meaningful only after some degree of belief. And more than that, there is no belief until there is faith. Later, we'll examine how scoffers are not exempt from this order. Scoffers also have faith, but unfortunately their faith is in a lie.

So, we are told in these verses that in the last days we will face scoffers who attempt to undermine the Word of God. We are told who these scoffers are and how we can know their scoffing is unjustified. Now we will examine the foundation of the scoffer's truths.

2. What Can We Know?

Now faith is the substance of things hoped for, the evidence of things not seen. For by it the elders obtained a good report. Through faith we understand that the worlds were framed by the word of God, so that things which are seen were not made of things which do appear.
Hebrews 11:1-3

The third verse here says that the world is not made of things that we see. This is in sharp contrast to the modern, uniformitarian view. Possibly the most interesting aspect of this verse is the question of why. Why was this statement made? Was there any previous generation that really cared that the world was not made from the materials we see that it is made of? Probably not. I can find no reason for God to record this verse except to assert, one more time, that the creation account in Genesis is correct and scoffers are wrong. It emphasizes that God cares quite a bit about His creation account. Perhaps we should also.

What Can We Know?

These verses tell us that our belief in the record that God has given us is the product of faith. Scoffers say that their beliefs are the product of proof and that proof is better than faith. There is a lot to be said in favor of proof. It is easy to have faith in a lie. Proof, by design, is intended to help us to avoid belief in erroneous facts. Proof is a rigorous process that scrutinizes information and conclusions for plausibility before they are accepted as truth.

So, how good is proof? How well does it protect us from belief in truths that are actually false? The scoffer seems to imply that it is infallible. Even if a few proofs turn out to be erroneous, the collected proofs of millions of people just can't be wrong. That sounds good, but is it true? Can millions of people collectively be wrong at the same time about the same thing? Even if they can, that doesn't mean that faith is better, does it?

Proof is a product of our modern intellectual pursuits. It has been developed to provide a more reliable access to truth than previous methods of reasoning and it can do just that. Does that make older modes of reasoning obsolete? Does proof make faith unnecessary? Our culture seems to take for granted that faith is only of value when proof isn't available.

Today it is generally recognized that the earth is very old and there was no flood of the scale recorded in Genesis. Many insist that there is consensus among scientists that this view is indisputable scientific fact. In contrast, II Peter 3 is a comparatively recent reaffirmation that the events recorded in Genesis are literal and that the generally recognized truths of today are not true at all.

Here we have two prominent accounts of our origin and it is necessarily true that at least one is substantially wrong. How do we know which? A person might adopt the attitude that we should always hold fast to the word of God, and I would not want to discourage anyone who thinks in that way. But I believe God did not make us mindless beings who are not expecting to think through the things we believe. God has made us active participants within creation and we are expected to behave accordingly. To that end, we can investigate this clash of beliefs and try to understand why it exists. In doing so, we become better able to *be ready always to give an answer to every man that asketh you a reason of the hope that is in you* (I Peter 3:15). We also become a corrective influence in the world.

What Can We Know?

So, how can highly intelligent and educated people be scoffers if the beliefs of scoffers are clearly wrong? How can we know that Genesis is accurate?

Objective Reality

Many of our beliefs in western culture are predicated on the existence of an absolute truth. Absolute truth is invariant throughout creation irrespective of time, place, and circumstance. Absolute truths are mutually reinforcing and never in conflict.

Necessarily, absolute truth requires an objective reality, a reality that is fully consistent with absolute truth. This reality is unique and something everyone has in common. Individually, we perceive objective reality differently and that creates differences of opinion about the nature of reality. These differences lead to conflict.

As our knowledge of absolute truth increases, our perception of objective reality improves. However, absolute truth is not easily discovered. It is a part of the objective reality that we do not all perceive in the same way. We are left with a paradox in which we understand objective reality with the knowledge of absolute truth, and our misunderstanding of objective reality prevents us from recognizing absolute truth, if

Objective Reality

we find it. If we try to be open-minded perhaps, we can learn new truths that improve our perceptions. Unfortunately, we may also learn new truths that are in fact invalid, and our perception grows worse.

Embedded in the post-modern way of thinking is the idea that objective reality is either non-existent or undiscoverable. Either way, the elusive nature of objective reality makes its pursuit futile. Consequently, the only reality we can know is our own personal perception of reality. By embracing this idea, we let perception *define* reality. Since no one has a strong grasp of objective reality, our perception is just as good as any other. Even better, we can change our perceptions with reasonable ease. Just imagine the reality you want, adjust your perception to match, and you can take control of your own personalized reality. Self improvement exercises frequently make use this technique. They can be helpful to those whose self perception is erroneously negative or counter productive. They also have the potential to develop new unproductive self perceptions such as egotism.

To some degree, influence is the effect of changing someone else's perception of reality. Today, you can even shop for a pre-packaged reality from many that are being offered in politics, economics, science, philosophy, and religion.

What Can We Know?

Having our own personal version of reality sort of works until something disturbs our chosen reality. A disturbance can be as personal as an encounter with someone who has chosen a reality in which they do harm to us or to what we consider important. Who gets to have what they want?

At least with objective reality, we could say that the person most closely aligned with that reality should have precedence. That takes us back to the original problem of discovering absolute truth. Without it, everyone is righteous in their own reality. Everyone outside of our reality is an evil doer. Proverbs 30:12 says this: *There is a generation that are pure in their own eyes, and yet is not washed from their filthiness.* That would describe a generation that only recognizes their own perception of reality in which they are the standard of righteousness.

Relative truth and perceived reality will not solve our problems, but they can take away what solutions we do have. What we really need is a strong understanding of objective reality, and that requires a knowledge of absolute truth, as much as we can get.

Irrefutable Truth

We believe many things to be true such as "the sun will rise in the morning". Will the sun rise in the morning? Probably. But just how sure are we? Is this fact *irrefutable?* If we mean that we know of no plausible reason why the sun will not rise in the morning, then the answer is yes, we know of no plausible cause that would refute the assertion. But the question remains, does there exist a reason for the sun not to rise in the morning that we are not aware of? We don't know and we can't expect to prove or disprove such a thing.

Before we can prove that something will not prevent the sun from rising in the morning, we need to identify what that something is. Maybe it's a big bang happening right in the middle of the sun, putting an end to it right away. Maybe it's an error in our understanding of physics and the sun explodes unexpectedly. If we succeed in proving that these events cannot happen, there are many, many more potential events that we have not identified, and therefore have not been proven to be harmless. Let's call the existence of such an unidentified event the *lurking effect*.

What Can We Know?

If our standard of truth only takes into account those things we already know, then we can possibly establish some irrefutable truths, for a while at least. From time to time, new knowledge does appear which does provide the necessary cause to refute previously irrefutable truths. Using this standard of truth, we do well to condition our truths as "irrefutably true sans plausible lurking effect". But we never actually do that. We just act surprised when one of our irrefutable truths turns out to be refuted.

Returning to the claims made by scoffers, their claim is that science can refute the second coming and that the creation and flood accounts in Genesis are not historically valid. God has identified the flood as the scoffer's lurking effect, so for the remainder of this discussion, I will use irrefutable truth to mean irrefutable in the presence of a lurking effect. This means that we can have a truth that we believe and consider to be irrefutable. If a previously unidentified event occurs and invalidates our truth, then the original belief in that truth is also considered to have been invalid. The implication is that the original belief in the infallibility of the truth was an error.

Knowledge and Reasoning

Our first method of acquiring knowledge is by observation. We see or otherwise sense (observe) things and incorporate that information into our collection of knowledge. What is recorded in our memory includes our interpretations of sensory information, not just the raw information itself. If we observe a person entering a room, we don't record that information like a camera. Instead, we assess the significance of what we are seeing. Is this a person? Do we know the person? Why is the person entering the room? Is the person's entry good, bad, or indeterminate?

The knowledge we collect is heavily processed before we add it to our collection. Once collected, that knowledge becomes fact even though it is a derivative of the actual observed information. Memories can be reconstructed from the interpreted information rather than the raw visual data. This can be problematic when the interpretation is erroneous. There isn't a lot we can do about that; our core source of knowledge is an interpretation of what we have sensed.

It is also possible to invent knowledge, which uses imagination. We are free to imagine any idea. The

What Can We Know?

result is knowledge although the value or quality of that knowledge may be suspect. Valuable inventions are often in part the product of imagination, invented knowledge. It is important that knowledge obtained in this way receive extra scrutiny before it is deemed valid. In science, this would be called a theory, and the theory would need supporting evidence before confidence is placed in the theory.

A third and very important source of knowledge is that knowledge that is derived from existing knowledge. This is the process of reasoning. There are many ways to go about reasoning. Often, our interpretations of observation take into account existing knowledge that is in some way related to the new observation. We make an observation and recognize that it fits into a pattern that has been established by previous observations. We can then derive additional knowledge about the observation by attributing the common elements of those past observations. This is a natural and effortless process for us. It is also subject to a lot of error. Just because an observation is familiar doesn't guarantee that our past experiences with similar observations are really applicable.

An old and well-known article of wisdom is that first impressions are very important. The first impression (memory) you make on another person will be used to interpret all future observations that person makes about you. If the impression is negative, future observations the other person makes regarding you will be negatively biased. It would take many positive impressions to overcome that one initial negative impression.

First impressions are powerful because they aren't in conflict with existing knowledge even though they are often made from woefully incomplete information. When additional and different information becomes available, we are reluctant to change the interpretations we made based on the first impression. The first impression becomes a bias that inhibits our ability to treat new information objectively.

We use some form of reasoning to validate invented knowledge. We can invent (imagine) a new idea, but then we evaluate that idea in the context of what we already know. If our idea is for a perpetual motion machine, we should immediately become skeptical of the idea based on our past experience with motion. Such ideas are pretty much always found to be erroneous.

It is important that we are able to associate the source of knowledge with the knowledge itself. A person who is unable to do so has a problem, as do the peo-

What Can We Know?

ple who meet them. If we keep in mind that we are using knowledge from a first impression, we can (partially) compensate for the poor quality of the knowledge that first impressions provide. A serious problem will exist if a person does not recognize when they are using memories reconstructed from dreams or other invented knowledge. They believe those memories are of real events. Consider the consequences of knowing a person who truly believes you have done all of the things that happened in their dreams or nightmares. Or if they just speculate that you have done this thing or that, and then come to truly believe that those things were real. Similarly, a powerful mechanism for manipulation is embedding knowledge into a person's memory (i.e., propaganda) while diluting their association with that information's source. People believe the knowledge they have without recognizing the weakness of the information's source.

All of these sources of knowledge are very unreliable. They would seem to supply us with knowledge that is just as likely to be useless as it is to be valuable, maybe more likely. We need to filter this muddy supply to obtain a cleaner supply of knowledge, and the filter we use is generally referred to as reason. It is the

Knowledge and Reasoning

process of justifying our belief that a piece of information is clean or contaminated.

There are two components needed to reason, those things we already know, and the processes that we can use to obtain new knowledge from that which we already have. Both components have the potential to be contaminated. A filter that is dirty on both sides does a poor job. Likewise, our ability to reason is impaired if we begin with contaminated knowledge. We need to obtain some clean knowledge that we can use to filter out the contaminates to obtain additional uncontaminated knowledge.

For simplicity, I will call these two components of reason facts and rules. Facts are the things we know and rules are the processes we use to obtain new facts from those we already have. In general, these facts may be true, false, or neither. Our belief in these facts may also be true, false, or neither. If neither, we usually attribute some qualitative degree of reliability to them as facts. My lottery ticket is a winner. That fact is usually true or false. It could however be neither if the ticket is a forgery. In this case, it isn't a lottery ticket at all, the information was dirty. If the drawing for the lottery has not yet occurred, the fact is at this time neither true nor false, but a probability; the likelihood of being true. We have rules that can give us that probability with a great deal of precision.

Reasoning based on experience is essentially inescapable, but it is also highly biased. Our experiences play heavily in how we interpret information. If we want to improve our objectivity and increase our confidence in the validity of our knowledge we need to find (maybe invent or imagine) a way to remove this and other kinds of bias from our reasoning. In the lottery ticket example, we would use statistics.

Logical reasoning has been developed to formalize reasoning processes in such a way that bias and error can be removed. Under the right conditions, it can provide a mechanism for error-free reasoning. Another process is the scientific method. It provides rules for acquisition and validation of knowledge, but is less formal than logic.

I Think Therefore I Am

Efforts to reason about our existence have been ongoing for the last few millennia. These efforts go beyond building or perpetuating a tradition of mythology. Instead they attempt to provide a plausible explanation for the universe that is independent of a fixed, preconceived narrative. This has been the work

I Think Therefore I Am

of philosophy. As philosophy has advanced, philosophers have become more demanding of the field, requiring more robust standards of reasoning. In recent centuries, methods of formalized reasoning have been developed with the intent to remove human bias and error from the process. If such bias and error is removed, the result should be something like an irrefutable truth.

We have found that we have more than one kind of truth, that which we believe true, or highly, probably true, and that which is irrefutably true. And since we can't count on the sunrise, we may start wondering just what truth might qualify as irrefutable.

The identification of an irrefutable truth turns out to be a hard question. It means finding a truth on which no adversary of that truth can cast any doubt. Since adversaries are free to speculate about a lurking effect that was not accounted for in a proof, it is a very, very hard question. Much intellectual effort has been put into solving this problem. In ancient times, the rigor applied to the problem was less than it is now. The reasons surely varied with political climate, the tools that were available, and their expectations.

The last reason is significant. Individuals in an environment in which no one is accustomed to having to justify a belief in some truth may not see the need for it. An example can be found in the Acts of the Apostles:

> *And when the townclerk had appeased the people, he said, Ye men of Ephesus, what man is there that knoweth not how that the city of the Ephesians is a worshipper of the great goddess Diana, and of the image which fell down from Jupiter?*
>
> *Seeing then that these things cannot be spoken against, ye ought to be quiet, and to do nothing rashly.*
> Acts 19:35-36

In Ephesus, the knowledge of Diana was assumed fact. The town clerk reminded the people of the truth of the goddess Diana and that it was known by everyone and therefore irrefutable. A pretty low standard of truth, but if you listen carefully you will find that this mode of reasoning hasn't changed at all. Today, when someone advocates for a decision or a position, it usually includes pointing out what everyone else thinks and does. Peer pressure is universal.

A notable example of an attempt at rigorously defined truth is presented in the *Method* by René Descartes in the seventeenth century. Descartes made the statement translated, "I think therefore I am." The problem Descartes was addressing is the

I Think Therefore I Am

problem of establishing some fact (any fact really) such that it could not be refuted. This not a trivial undertaking and an important part of Descartes' work. So important that it has become a widely recognized quotation to this day. So, what does it mean? He is claiming that he exists and that his existence is proven by the fact that he can think (e.g., contemplate his existence). If he can think, he surely must exist, and if he doesn't exist, then he couldn't possibly be thinking. That is all pretty reasonable, but is it true? If we say that it is true, what reason can we give for thinking so? We are thinking too! We now have more knowledge than Descartes since we know that we exist, and we have obtained the knowledge that Descartes exists.

But does the sound of music prove the existence of a musician? We can trace the sound, but we may only find a machine rather than a musician. Likewise, if we trace the origin of thought, do we necessarily find ourselves, or even a person? With music we can make a credible case that the sound of music does prove the existence of a musician, but not that the musician is present or presently producing the music. So, can thought establish the existence of a thinker without proving that the thinker is thinking synchronously with the observed thought? A thinker might stop thinking, or even stop existing while the thoughts themselves persist, like an echo or a recording?

We can record thoughts on paper. Is there more to thinking than the medium in which they are found? We can read someone's thoughts from a paper record, and now those same thoughts are our thoughts, recreated from paper. Does this make those paper thoughts more legitimate? Do thoughts recorded on paper prove the prior existence of a person who thought them? If so, how is it proof? Because thoughts "don't just happen"? If we say that is true, we have opened Pandora's box. We admit that there is some physical representation of thoughts that can prove the existence of a person who thinks. How about DNA?

What if thoughts recorded on paper do not prove the existence of a thinking person who produced them? Then what we observe as ourselves thinking might actually be thoughts recorded in some medium. We now say that such a recording does not prove the existence of a thinking person. In this case, we are thinking, but that is just our thoughts recorded in some medium which we no longer believe sufficient to prove the existence of a thinker. So, we don't actually exist even though our recorded thoughts think we do.

If Descartes is wrong, and it is possible to think without existing, then we can also think about his assumption, agree with it, and yet we don't exist either. Indeed, we didn't think any of this until we read what Descartes wrote. Maybe we have more in common with a music box than a thinking person.

If we pursue this hard enough, we likely begin to question the definition of existence and of thought. As we go down that road Descartes' assertion starts to lose its utility as our terms lose the definitions we once thought they had.

Philosophers have presented a number of critiques of Descartes' work that point out a number of its shortcomings. I simplify and summarize a few of them here:

- If Descartes is doubting his own existence, how sure can he be that he would recognize thinking if he was in fact doing it?
  This calls into question one of our most fundamental definitions and observations—that there is thinking and thinking is in progress. If we can't even believe that with confidence, would any observation be satisfactory?

What Can We Know?

- Not much is actually being said since the person must exist for thinking to exist, so the conclusion says very little.

  In this case, we accept that thinking can only be done by a person who exists. This is a shared assumption that must be true in order for Descartes' statement to be true. So, Descartes isn't saying anything that isn't already known by those who share his assumption, except possibly adding that he, Descartes, can think. Those who do not share his assumption will not be convinced.

- We tend to define thinking as an activity of a person. How do we know thinking isn't self-sustainable, i.e., no person needed to do the thinking? How do we know thinking (consciousness) is unique to a person (as we define person)? How do we know there are any persons other than ourselves? Perhaps we have observed thinking, how do we know we aren't observing someone else thinking?

We can do a lot of thinking just trying to figure out if we are thinking, and if thinking can be used to conclude that we exist, and if the whole process isn't rather trivial. In the end, was anything accomplished? Perhaps this: We aren't very good at knowing anything that someone can't dispute.

The point I want to make here is that our facts should be considered finitely reliable. We can't really prove that they are true to the extent that we know no one will ever be able to refute them. Our most basic assumptions always seem to crumble into additional, even more basic assumptions.

Perhaps we can summarize the situation this way: Any attempt to establish a fundamental fact or truth always produces an assumption. The validity of the fundamental assumption depends on additional assumptions (it wasn't fundamental after all). The consequent endless chain of assumptions makes reasoning with the fundamental fact or truth infinitely linear (like circular reasoning over an infinite radius) so that no truly definitive conclusion can be reached.

This doesn't mean that our facts are invalid, just that they aren't demonstrably infallible. When we believe in the validity of a fact or assumption, there is always an element of *faith* involved.

Logical Reasoning

So why not avoid muddy assumptions altogether and just proceed with a sterile platform of theorems and proofs and such? You can try, but you won't succeed. No matter what idea you may want to express, there must be some context in which to express it. And that context is assumed—it must be. So in formal reasoning, it is recognized that there is a need to begin with assumptions and that the reasoning process is made much more rigorous if all assumptions are explicit.

Reasoning from such a set of assumptions we can find additional facts—facts that must be true given the initial assumptions. When we begin with different assumptions, we derive different facts. Not necessarily conflicting facts, just different facts.

Logical reasoning was developed as a formal way to objectively derive truths from known facts (e.g., axioms). From time to time, you may have heard that some item of knowledge is axiomatic. That is just stating that the knowledge is accepted as true without proof or justification. It is not an error to use axioms—it is inescapable.

A substantial portion of modern mathematics is devoted to systematized development of these ideas and much of this field falls under the heading *logic*. A useful product of these efforts is the recognition that the axioms can be inconsistent. Inconsistency means that some proposition can be both proven and refuted with the set of axioms—a *contradiction*. Moreover, if the axioms are inconsistent, any proposition can be proven, which makes the whole process of reasoning useless. Obviously then, it is important that we always work with a consistent set of axioms. We'll see that this goal is not provably achievable.

In addition to a consistent set of axioms, we must make inferences that are valid, meaning that the inferences do not introduce a contradiction. It is important that we use rules of inference that are valid, just as the axioms must be consistent, but how do we know the rules are valid? Any attempt to formalize this process necessarily encounters a chicken-and-egg problem.

We need a set of valid rules to prove the rules are valid. We address this problem by creating an initial set of rules that are so basic, unambiguous, and in some sense "obvious" that we do not believe we can be wrong in concluding that they are, in fact, valid. Every effort is made to find some inconsistency, and if none is found, a general agreement can be reached that the rules are valid. For example there was a time when a rule such as "what goes up must come down" would have been generally agreeable. We now know that this rule is not strictly true.

What Can We Know?

An important element in this process is that if any *counter example* can be provided (an example of a contradiction), the system of axioms and inferences is rejected. The spacecraft Voyager has left the solar system and it will not be coming back. It serves as a counter example to the rule of "what goes up...".

Thorough and meticulous implementation of this process has yielded systems of logic that are quite reliable. I think it is fair to say that these systems were found to be quite reliable long ago and have been subject to many improvements since.

The field of logic has been developed to support our reasoning efforts. Today, the field of logic is vast, looking at the subject from many perspectives and struggling with various difficult issues. A most-critical aspect of this work for our immediate purpose is the introspective products of the field of logic. Among these products are those that look to formalize and then automate the process of reasoning. There have been two particularly interesting outcomes of this work. First, it is not feasible to fully automate the reasoning process. If this were not true, we would be able to delegate the job of reasoning to a machine (a computer as we know them today). Second, we are limited in our ability to formally (mechanically) verify the correctness of our systems of logic.

So, why bring all of this up? We would like to establish the boundary (if any) of what is possible for us to know and learn. These limitations will not only apply to ourselves, but to scoffers as well. Logic has several properties that make it interesting in this regard. Logic is developed specifically for purposes of this kind. It is as simple as possible for its intended purpose to minimize the potential for error. Unlike the natural sciences (which are discussed later), no external constraints are imposed. There can be no lurking effects. The logician is free to include or restrict the content of a system of reasoning as the logician sees fit. In a sense, the logician creates his very own universe, and within that universe, constructs a set of facts and rules. The logician strives to create a universe such that it is considered, in some way, "sane" to his peers. Consistency is a common criterion and sometimes utility is as well. With all of this freedom to define the domain in which reasoning occurs, and with extensive introspection, how have logicians fared?

What Can We Know?

Incompleteness

Mathematicians aren't so constrained as Descartes. They are in effect constructing their own universe where truth is whatever the mathematician says it is. Does this solve the problem?

If we want to credibly establish an irrefutable fact, we will need to prove the factualness of the assertion of fact. Proof needs a degree of formality to enable us to apply a commonly accepted standard of reason to the process of proof so that an agreement can be reached regarding the validity of the poof and to remove potential lurking effects. Formalization of the proof or reasoning process begins with the assertion to be proved and the assumptions that are being made. From there, the reasoning process can begin to draw conclusions that must be true given the assumptions. At no time is the validity of the assumptions questioned. No meaningful reasoning can be made unless all assumptions are valid. Assumptions must not only be valid individually, but together they must be consistent—meaning, they never lead to contradictory conclusions.

How do we know a set of axioms are consistent? We might try to prove that our axioms are consistent the same way we prove any other assertion. In the early

Incompleteness

20th century, Kurt Gödel developed his Incompleteness Theorems. A simplified statement of the second of these theorems is that a consistent system of axioms (assumptions) cannot prove its own consistency. You are free to create a second set of axioms within which you can prove the consistency of the first, but the second set of axioms cannot prove their own consistency. If the second set of axioms is inconsistent, the proof of consistency for the first set is invalidated. Obviously, trying to prove consistency for the second set of axioms by creating a third will not solve our dilemma.

The result is that within the scope of applicability of Gödel's theorems, no proof is provably irrefutable. This Catch-22 that prevents us from proving the consistency of a set of axioms makes it so. That scope of applicability is defined by the axioms of Gödel's proof which are, of course, also not proven to be consistent. This scope of applicability is very broad and may well prevent an ultimate proof of consistency for all purposes. If true, our most powerful means of reasoning is now known to be unable to provide irrefutable truth.

If we can't prove a set of axioms to be consistent, we must by other means determine the consistency of our axioms. These other means cannot be formal

What Can We Know?

(per Gödel), so they are informal and subject to the bias of the person formulating the axioms. Mitigation of this bias is managed by a peer review of the axioms. If the peers agree that the axioms are sound, or at least they can find no contradiction, the axioms are accepted until such time as a flaw is discovered. There is no remedy for peers that share a common bias.

So, the consistency of the axioms is determined by our confidence in our own ability to informally reason that they are. You might say that this requires a degree of faith in the skill of the peers.

The prophet Jeremiah had this to say about our ability to reason: *The heart is deceitful above all things, and desperately wicked: who can know it?* (Jeremiah 17:9, KJV) He is saying that even our best intentions can be defeated—not by an adversary, but by our own weaknesses. If you don't believe this, you must have a difficult time explaining how people can seem so sincere in their beliefs about our origin (uniformitarianism vs catastrophism) without accusing one side or the other of malevolent intent. You can't blame it on stupidity; there are very intelligent people on both sides of the debate. Jeremiah said deceit is resident in the heart—everyone's heart. It is useful to think of the reasoning tools that have been developed in philosophy as an attempt to counter the deceitful heart and arrive at a valid truth, even when it is a different truth than we expected or wanted.

Mathematics provides us with our most powerful means of establishing the truth of some asserted fact, primarily because modern mathematics has been constructed (or retrofitted) for this purpose. The mathematician is not constrained by observation or any preconceived reality, but is free to make any assumptions deemed necessary to accomplish his ends. Even so, we find that with this flexibility of context, the mathematician is ultimately constrained in his ability to prove statements with absolute irrefutability. Mathematicians, too, exercise some degree of faith in the product of their efforts.

What Can We Learn?

At the beginning of the 20th century, there was a goal within the mathematics community to automate the process of proving theorems. Mathematicians would have a theorem that they wanted to prove or disprove, but the process was time consuming and unreliable. There was no way to know how long the process would take. If a step-by-step procedure (called an algorithm) could be developed for the process, the

What Can We Know?

job of constructing proofs could be handed off to assistants who would follow the set of instructions and produce the desired result. Today, we would use a computer to carry out the instructions.

Much effort was put into achieving this goal, without success. Alan Turing was a mathematician looking into the problem who took an alternate approach. First, he created a definition of what it meant to perform a computation, which is to say, what are the instructions you are allowed to give to your assistant. This outcome, often labeled the Church-Turing Thesis, captures exactly those actions an assistant can perform deterministically. According to the thesis, any action that is not included cannot be guaranteed to be (humanly) performable.

Using his definition of instructions that can be used to create an algorithm (known as the Turing machine), Turing proceeded to show that a mathematical problem, now known as the halting problem, could not be deterministically answered. A Turing machine can solve some halting problems but not all. The significance of Turing's finding is that there are problems we cannot solve with assurance.

Turing's results can be invalidated if a more powerful definition of computation can be found. Much ef-

What Can We Learn?

fort has been put into finding such a definition but none has been identified. Turing's machine remains the standard by which all computing machinery is measured. If a more powerful definition of computation can be found it would likely lead to more powerful computers. Such a find would be priceless, and maybe economically devastating as well.

Turing's results do not prohibit mathematicians from achieving some desired outcome, it only prevents us from building a machine to obtain those outcomes in a deterministic way. Asking a computer to answer such a question may result in an immediate answer or it may result in waiting forever for an answer that will never come. Today, there are many programs that do address such problems and our expectations are adjusted by the knowledge that we may be asking more from our machines than they can be expected to produce.

Are humans exempt from Turing's results? At the time Turing developed his theories, computers as we know them today did not exist. Automated computation meant giving your algorithm to an assistant. Turing's results were developed as a limitation on what humans can achieve. As a result, the problems that automated computation intended to render easy remain difficult.

What Can We Know?

The mathematicians' desire to put their questions into a machine (literal or a human acting as a machine), turn the crank and have answers pop out, is for now a broken dream. It will remain so for as long as Turing's definition of computation holds. What do we do when we want to know the answer to a question that is outside the bounds of "Turing computability"? We try. Maybe we get lucky, maybe we don't. We may never have an answer for some of our questions.

Does it matter? Even when we aren't concerned with lurking effects, we appear to be limited in what we can know and also in what we can discover.

Proof in the Natural Sciences

Within the natural sciences proof is a little different. These scientists attempt to describe the world we find ourselves in, a process that must begin with observation. From these observations, they deduce principles that explain why and how these observations come to be.

Sometimes, and more often as science has become more highly developed, the observations cannot be made directly. In this case, observations are made that suggest the existence of some unobserved el-

Proof in the Natural Sciences

ement whose existence escapes our direct observation. Now, the only reason we have for believing in the existence of this invisible element is that its existence is needed to explain what we can observe. For example, we can theorize the existence of a virus before we have the capability of building a microscope that can see the virus directly. The existence of the virus does a pretty good job of explaining the spread of diseases that are transmitted by contact with an infected person. We cannot observe the transfer, only the effect.

So, the process of proof in the natural sciences is to make observations and formulate a credible theory explaining the observations given what is currently known and believed. This is a very precarious process because it can and does yield many possible and competing theories that are contaminated by the biases of the scientist. To reinforce or discredit these theories and hopefully come to a single correct theory, scientists devise experiments. These experiments manipulate the subject that is being studied to produce new and different observations, or sometimes, to produce no different observation. A valid theory is expected to predict these new observations given the manipulations that are made. If new observations and theoretical predictions are the same confidence in the theory is reinforced. If they are not the same, either the theory or the experimental process is flawed. If no flaw is found in the experiment, the theory must be revised to account for the new observations or it should be discarded. Ideally, this is how scientific investigation is done.

Modern scientific work is not this easy. The tools and institutions that have been constructed to perform scientific experiments yield a large quantity of observations. Making these observations is a comparatively easy job compared to that of explaining the process behind those observations. Development of theories becomes more complex as the increase in observations yields conflicting results. When no fault can be found in experimental methods, it is the theory that must be addressed. This, too, is a simplification. Just because we identify a need to revise a theory to account for a new observation doesn't mean that it is evident, just what kind of revision is appropriate or adequate. Over time, unexplained observations tend to accumulate because no theory has been found that is capable of explaining all observations. Now the natural scientist has a problem. Observation and theory disagree and no flaw can be identified in the experimental processes that produced the observations. If the theory is considered discredited,

Proof in the Natural Sciences

then the scientist has no theory at all. If the theory is not discredited, the scientist proceeds from a position reasonably believed to be wrong. Not a good way to advance science.

What to do? We can classify a promising but problematic theory as a "working theory", meaning that it is recognized to have problems, yet scientists continue to use it as a platform to study the problems while they develop a new or revised theory that will replace it. This is really the only way to address the problematic theory, but additional problems remain. Continued research can result in additional supporting observations, and maybe a few contradictory observations as well, while failing to suggest a better theory. The working theory just persists with a growing body of supporting and conflicting evidence. Now, what? Ideally, the working theory remains just that—a working theory. It is tempting to accept the working theory as substantially correct with some caveats. Scientific research continues, predicated on the acceptance of a theory that is known to conflict with observation.

What does this mean to us? At the very least, we should understand that proof in the context of the natural sciences does not mean the same thing that it does in mathematics. Relying solely on observation, we often have to settle for those observations we are able to make rather than the observations we would like to make. And a theory that describes an observation is often just one of several, or many theories that explain the same observation. Even if there is just one theory explaining an observation, that does not mean that no other theory is possible, just that none have been found (a lurking theory). In the best case, where only one theory is known and is in agreement with all observations, there remains the possibility that the next observation will be conflicting or even discrediting. This would be a lurking observation.

As has been found in mathematics, so it is with the natural sciences—absolute proof is elusive at best. When a scientist asserts a fact, it usually means that the observations and theories are such that the scientist is convinced of the fact's validity. Other scientists may or may not be convinced and no one can honestly say with certainty that the fact is valid. Does it matter? We should always remember that scientific fact is subject to the standard of proof that each scientist has adopted. What one scientist considers solid proof may seem pretty weak to another, or to us. Additionally, when a scientist takes action on the facts they have discovered, they are exercising faith in those facts, consciously or not.

Occam's Razor

At the vergence of logic, observation, and statistics, we find a principle of reasoning known as Occam's razor. Named after 14th century philosopher William of Ockham, it is translated, "Plurality ought never be posited without necessity." Isaac Newton expressed the idea as, "We are to admit no more causes of natural things than such as are both true and sufficient to explain their appearances." In this case, true would mean not refuted.

Occam's razor has utility in science. When multiple theories are posed to explain a common set of observations, the simpler theory is the theory most likely to be correct. In this context, simpler means the theory with the fewest assumptions. The logic behind this principle is easy to understand. Each assumption made in a theory carries the risk (has a probability) of being found in error or in conflict with another assumption. Since the probability of an assumption being faulty cannot in general be quantified, we assign equal probability to all assumptions. The the-

What Can We Know?

ory with the fewest such assumptions would have the lowest probability of being incorrect.

Occam's razor is a general principle that is brought to bear after other means of discriminating among theories have been applied. There is no assurance that a simpler theory is correct or that more complex theories are wrong. It is used in intellectual pursuits to point us in the direction that is most likely to yield useful results.

Does it matter? Occam's razor is sometimes used to support creation as an explanation of origins. This can spark a strong response by some scientists who claim it is an invalid use of the principle. We should probably be familiar with its use in this context.

Does the existence of a creator provide the simplest explanation for our origin? It's pretty simple, as it has just one assumption—that we are created. An assumption that cannot be refuted. We can find some observation to support this theory, such as the fact that in all of recorded human experience, no originally new thing has ever been observed except that which was created (i.e., we created). Everything that exists is the propagation of what came before (was already existing). We might identify a few new things that we have made ourselves, but those things are

Occam's Razor

still created, not spontaneously appearing. We could even bring uniformitarianism to bear in this context and claim that a spontaneously appearing universe is improbable, the universe has to be the product of a pre-existing universe-maker. What does a universe-maker look like? Based on our experience, only intelligence can create something original.

An important argument against the use of Occam's razor is that it does not advance scientific inquiry. That is certainly true. In any investigation into the physical world, we can always win the simplicity game by saying *God did it*. With the phenomena now explained, we can conclude our investigation, science is not needed. Scientists say that isn't science and there is much truth in that. Science is the study of processes at work *in* the universe. If the origin of the processes is not the subject of study the scientist can be (and has been) productive without contemplating the origin of the process.

Another argument is that science and God are antithetical. I have seen no justification for this beyond the personal unbelief of the individual scientist. If the goal of science is to expand human knowledge, you would expect that there is no more important knowledge that could be obtained than that of the person who created us, or just that we were indeed created.

What Can We Know?

Yet, there are many scientists who insist that an investigation into this possibility has no place in science. There have been important scientists who suggest that life on earth was placed here by an alien civilization. They are willing to accept the possibility of an alien race that has never been observed, yet reject a creator on the same basis.

Many scientists insist that God exists outside the scope of science. I'm not sure that is the best approach to take, but just what is or is not a suitable topic for study is subjective. Less subjective, in my opinion, is the utility in the application of science to the study of the origin of the universe. This subject ventures so far outside of human experience as to make it incomprehensible. It must contemplate the non-existence of both space and time. Virtually all of the objective tools available to the scientist are unavailable in this effort. In this realm, with theories of spontaneous creation being built entirely on speculation, the idea that the universe was deliberately created has as much merit as any other. And in this context, Occam's razor does indeed apply.

Faith is Universal

It seems that it is an inescapable fact that there is no truth so well established that we can believe it without first exercising faith. We can justify such faith by pointing to the skill of scientists advocating in favor of their conclusions. We can justify our faith, saying that human weaknesses are not so great that a million scientists can all suffer the same bias and error at the same time. Whatever we use to justify our faith, it is still a choice, a decision that we make as individuals. We decide what we are going to believe—it cannot be imposed by virtue of an infallible logic or proof.

Is proof better than faith? Proof cannot displace faith, so the answer is clearly no. Is proof of no value? Definitely not. Proof, and the processes that produce it, are excellent tools that help us to understand the faith that we ultimately reach. They allow us to understand why we have faith and why we do not. This understanding can be very helpful when we encounter someone who tells us our faith is ridiculous. We all know of people whose faith is indeed ridiculous, at least to us. When our own faith is challenged, we need to be able to explain, to ourselves at least, why we have *this* faith.

The verses that started this chapter tell us that it is by our faith that we understand the truth. Not reason, not science, not logic. We can do all of those things and still reach the wrong understanding if our faith is wrong. This is how scoffers get it wrong. They can be very intelligent, and they may be very diligent in their efforts to obtain a legitimate truth, but unless their faith is with God, they can't reach His truth. It is the creator's truth—the one truth that matters.

Conclusion

Scoffers have concluded that God is dead and that they have incontrovertible proof. So far, we have discovered two things. We have seen that scoffers, like all humans, do not possess the means to provide such incontrovertible proof. Also, this "dead God" has anticipated the scoffer's very existence, his philosophy, and his means of proof. He has provided for the refutation of the scoffer's ideas and reminded us that it is the scoffer who is destined to die. Have we proven the claims of the scoffers to be invalid? We ourselves are not able to do so. What I have attempted to show is that the claims of scoffers are the product of their faith, and that those claims are open to refutation. At this point, it may seem that the believer stands on equal footing with the scoffer,

Conclusion

and that the prospect for finding truth is pretty bleak. Next we address this state of affairs and see that the believer and the scoffer are not equal at all.

3. What Can We Believe?

Limited Utility of Proof

Ideally, proof would exclude any theory that is in conflict with a theory that has been proven. If two conflicting theories are both proven there is a problem with at least one of the proofs. For small theories (theories about simple things), maybe an exclusive proof is possible. Larger theories such as a theory of origins never seem to meet this ideal. Usually, any one person does recognize only one proof among several that conflict. Although not often explicitly stated in this way, the scoffer's rejection of the creation and flood events described in the Bible may be made on this basis. The scoffer has already deemed his own theory proven and so feels confident in rejecting all conflicting theories.

Our use of the term "proof" is often very careless. Theories are considered proven, even when there is much that the theory does not address satisfactorily.

What Can We Believe?

Because of this, two theories that partially explain observation may coexist, each with its own adherents who believe their theory to be proven. It would be better to acknowledge that the support for each theory falls short of "proof".

So, proof tends to be a rather all or nothing concept. If we are earnest in our pursuit of truth, we may come to the realization that proof is often a poor tool for our purposes. When we discover a "proof", there is little incentive for further investigation into the validity of the proven theory. A faulty theory that is considered to be proven is seldom discredited by its proponents, but rather by its detractors. A person who just wants to know the truth would do well to avoid being such an overzealous proponent.

A more productive approach would be to evaluate theories, especially theories with sincere critics, on the basis of how adequate they are to explain observation. Our purpose in doing so is to avoid "target fixation", where a person is focused on proving one theory and disproving another such that they lose objectivity.

Adequacy can be considered a valuation on a scale of zero to fully adequate. It can also contemplate the degree of harmony between theory and observation, such as theory explains observation, theory cannot (yet) explain observation, and theory contradicts observation. This approach to the evaluation of theories should help us to objectively evaluate not just a theory we believe (or want to believe) to be false, but also a theory we believe (or want to believe) to be true.

Characterizing theories on the basis of adequacy can help us to remain cognizant that each theory does have pros and cons, support and criticism. We can still draw conclusions, but hopefully we do so with a clearer understanding of how we reached our conclusions and just how firm our justification is for those conclusions.

While this may sound good, it is not easy to do in practice. We are still subject to the constraints of Jeremiah 17:9—we are still not able to be as objective as we want to be, even though we try. I do think, however, that at this time believers are in a better position than scoffers to put this proposal into practice. For the scoffer, rejecting creation is easy. It is easy for the deceitful heart to take comfort in the consensus opinion. It helps that we can say "all real/serious/legitimate scientists believe ..." to assure ourselves that we have reached the correct conclusion, even though it is the evidence that should matter.

What Can We Believe?

Christians are swimming against the current and are easily challenged. If a Christian wants reason to believe that his faith is justified, rather than repaying insult with insult, he must address the criticism of scoffers. The deceitful heart has a more difficult time finding comfort in this.

Since much of this book is focused on scoffers and their error, do note that I am not suggesting that scoffers be less dogmatic. That would be futile. Rather, I suggest that the rest of us have a solid understanding of our own beliefs. If we place our faith in weak arguments, our faith is easily defeated, even with counter arguments that are themselves weak. If we understand the strength of our arguments and their counter arguments, we should be able to understand why we believe what we do. We are able to take control of our beliefs and the changes we make to our beliefs.

Something More

In the last chapter, I explored the extent to which we humans are able to discover and validate facts and truth using only our own powers of observation and reason. The conclusion was that to the best of our understanding, we are finite in our ability to learn,

Something More

know, and understand. In the end, we must always exercise some degree of faith when we decide to believe in the validity of some fact or truth. Absolute truth is elusive.

People vary in what they require from some claim of truth before they place their faith in it. Internet scams use surprisingly sophisticated methods to identify people willing to believe unlikely stories with no supporting evidence to become victims of their fraudulent activities. For example the "Nigerian prince" email scam has been around for years and is widely recognized. By design it is very poorly disguised for the purpose of identifying potential victims that are easily seduced.

More modern variations utilize social engineering to lower the threshold of naivete needed on the part of the victim. A few years ago I received an example of this newer type of email scam. It was sent to me by name from someone I work with to my work email. It included details of our work processes and said that the coworker was very busy and needed a favor. It was disturbing to see how much slower my "scam reflex" was this time.

If absolute truth is indiscernible, is there any point in trying? Does it matter? Thus far, I may have made the

What Can We Believe?

outlook for discovering truth seem bleak. Well, for the scoffer, that is true. What has been discussed is all that he has. This chapter discusses what the scoffer does not have.

A point of focus in this work has been to address the claims being made by scoffers. Christians are faced with conflicting claims: The claims of scoffers and the claims of God. Obviously, we can just side with the creator over scoffers, that isn't as unreasonable as scoffers may say it is. Is that really all we have? Is there nothing more that we can say and think about this conflict of claims?

If we are to use reason to resolve these conflicting claims, we need to choose a basis for reasoning that is suitable to make the necessary discernment. The choice we make here will be largely responsible for the outcome of our efforts. The approach we take to reasoning about a subject may lead to a strong conclusion or a weak conclusion. If we are able to identify our conclusions as weak, we do well to start over, taking a different and hopefully better approach.

The prophecy of II Peter 3 points us to one such basis for reasoning about our origin, namely geology. This basis is sufficient to refute scoffers, but that is about all. The accounts recorded in Genesis when coupled with scientific research can provide a compelling case for our creation by God as recorded in the Bible. And if that is true, then there is a strong case to believe everything else recorded in the Bible also.

Skeptics

But in addition to scoffers, there are others who dispute God's authenticity. Many such people claim as a basis for their "skepticism", the lack of any reason to believe that any god created us, much less the God of the Bible. Or maybe they hold that we might have been created, but there is no reason to believe that the God of the Bible is the one who is responsible. Either way, they have excused themselves from the burden of complying with God's standards. There is a sense in which these critics, too, can be countered with the combination of the accounts of Genesis and relevant scientific research.

I think that much, if not all, of the claims of skeptics can be collected under the general umbrella of an *illusion of a creator*. That is, we have this ancestral need for God, so our minds distort our perceptions such that we see proof of God where there is none. Obviously, this same argument can be used against skeptics and doing so descends into a food fight of faiths. The skeptic might say something to the effect that our ancestral legacy is full of religious beliefs which we can agree are purely illusion. It is probable, therefore, that all religion is illusion. That is a pretty good argument I think—one I want to take seriously.

As an aside, let me say I do not consider this to be a problem with respect to salvation. We are told that, *My sheep hear my voice, and I know them, and they follow me* (I John 10:27).

What basis of reason can be used to address such a claim if it is being made by a skeptic? Genesis won't help us here; the skeptic has said that we are imagining the support for Genesis because of an inherited (evolutionarily primitive) bias that prevents us from reasoning clearly. The skeptic is the one who has moved beyond these primitive biases to recognize them for what they really are. Well, yikes! If we are sincere in our wish to know the truth, this could be perplexing.

The Search

We need to approach the issues raised by our skeptics with a basis for reasoning capable of reaching conclusions that, we at least, find as strong as those the skeptic has. Of course, we really want the strongest possible conclusions, but we have no way of knowing when we have found them. So, we must be content with the strongest we are able to find.

I begin by suggesting that underlying the arguments of scoffers, skeptics, and others who say there is no creator, or that if there is a creator, we don't know who that might be, is this fundamental if unspoken claim: *There is no knowable creator and you can't show credible evidence that there is.* Pretty much any argument against the literal God as described in the Bible would need to include this as an axiom or try to prove it as a conclusion. What we found in Chapter 2 does seem to support this claim. Is there something we can say to that? Is this the best we can do and reason cannot help the believer at all?

If we are going to address effectively the claims of scoffers and skeptics, we need to explore these claims as best we can. That is, we need to explore the idea that we can't prove that there is a creator.

What can we say about a creator? By definition, He is the creator, therefore His credentials are creation itself. What is His creation? The creation I am going to consider is all of the known universe, what is observable, directly or indirectly. That would include not just the things we can see and feel, but also time and space. I choose this definition because, to the best of our knowledge, everything that is observable has some kind of origin. A skeptic may say that the same reasoning applies to God—He must have an origin. In my view at least, the fallacy in this argument is that the rules we have observed within creation (e.g., that things have origins) may not apply outside creation.

These definitions give us an unbounded God, meaning that we can say that such a creator is not confined in space or time since both are observable elements of the universe and therefore are part of the creation. If the creator is not so confined, then our powers of observation are useless for discovering this person. We can't see or otherwise detect the creator other than the one indirect observation: "I observe the creation and deduce that there is/was a creator." This doesn't help much to address skeptics who might say: "I observe a self-creating/sustaining universe and no evidence of anything outside of it." Perhaps skeptics would not like having me attribute such arguments to them, but I personally find them more convincing than anything I have actually heard from a skeptic.

I don't really buy the argument that the observed universe has the appearance of being self-creating or

The Search

sustaining. There are some pretty good observations that indicate the universe is not the well-oiled evolution machine it appears to be.

In a very real sense, the skeptic has a point. If God exists outside all observable artifacts, there is nothing that we can do to detect Him. Our eyes and ears can't reach outside the universe to where he can be found. We can't send the creator an email or text message, we don't know his address. He is as invisible as anything could ever be. At this point, we are still believing on faith. Either faith that the existence of a creation is evidence of a creator or that the lack of an observed creator is evidence that no creator exists. God has said that His creation is the proof of Him. I can find this argument satisfactory even if the skeptic doesn't. Let's keep looking and see what else we might find that addresses the skeptic.

So, a creator would exist beyond creation and is therefore unobservable from within the creation. This is *our* limitation. Nothing prevents the creator from communicating with us. The creator necessarily does not share our limitations. The question we need to be asking ourselves is this: *Has the creator made contact with us?* This, I think, will be a much more fruitful line of thinking.

What Can We Believe?

Contrary to what many scoffers and scientists may say, I do not think that the question, has the/a creator contacted us, to be unsuitable for scientific inquiry. Regardless, it seems that the question is left to be explored as a religious and philosophical field of investigation.

If the creator has made legitimate contact with creation, then someone knows about it; otherwise, it isn't contact. There are people and religions that claim to represent contact from the creator. The job of determining if such contact has actually been made is the job of sifting through the various claims looking for the most valid claim. Then we evaluate that claim.

I propose the following criteria to evaluate a claim of contact with the creator:

1. Any religion that does not include a creator does not contribute to the search for the creator.
2. The creator must have an existence outside of creation (time and space), otherwise he cannot be the creator.
3. Contact made earlier in the timeline of creation is stronger than contact made later. (i.e., If the creator waits until recently to communicate

with his creation, we should ask, why? Why not communicate with people as soon as they are created? Were the ancients just boring?)

4. An explanation of who the creator is, is stronger than having no such explanation.
5. An explanation of the creation event is stronger than having no such explanation.
6. Consistency in the content of communication is stronger than inconsistency.

It is never acceptable to evaluate (or judge) the creator by human standards. We might theorize that creation would reflect the standards of a creator. Such a theory is just conjecture since it is making assumptions (or worse, failing to make assumptions) about why we were created. There is no assurance that a creator will meet these criteria, but this is a place to start. If our search finds nothing, we can adjust our criteria and try again. We must begin the search somewhere, and I have selected these criteria using my best judgment and what knowledge I have at my disposal.

I do not intend to take time and space here to attempt a survey of claims of contact from a creator. Feel free to take on this task—I would be interested in your findings. Instead, I have set a framework in which such claims can be measured, and I will use

What Can We Believe?

that framework to evaluate what I see as the best available description of contact from our creator, the Bible.

Items 1 and 2 are simple and they eliminate many claims from this search. Starting with the Old Testament, we have the most detailed account of creation that is available to us from any source. It begins from the beginning (the beginning of time) with contact between creator and created occurring immediately after beings were created that were capable of communication. That satisfies criteria 3 and 5. There has been ongoing communication since that time, much of which is written explaining who God is and what he expects from us.

Information about the nature of the creator (God) is found throughout the Bible, satisfying criterion 4. Communication has been ongoing from the beginning in a process of progressive revelation, meaning that the details of the creator's plans and motivations have been communicated in phases that are building toward a climactic conclusion. This satisfies criterion 6.

A consistent theme in the Bible has been a rigid standard of righteousness and judgment harmonized with compassion and forgiveness. This is not something we expect to encounter elsewhere. Instead, we find unrighteousness (gods whose behavior is no better than human), unyielding judgment (gods who cannot be pleased), or gods without standards, they forgive on a whim, making a mockery of their own standards of right and wrong. The God of the Bible claims to be perfect in righteousness, but forgives those who ask for it. These seemingly contradictory attributes are reconciled by God Himself enduring the unbearable consequences of the sin that He has forgiven. In this way, the demands of righteousness are satisfied: All sins are offset with punishment, either by the one who committed the sin or by a satisfactory and volunteer substitute. Simultaneously, forgiveness is freely available to those who ask to be forgiven from the one person able to pay the price of sin in their place.

It is true that a creator is under no obligation to be righteous or to establish standards of right and wrong. But if he says he does, we should look for consistency. If we don't find it, we should wonder why a creator so powerful as to create the entire universe can't manage to be consistent in his word and deed.

I have not provided a survey of how the various religions compare on these criteria. Such a comparison can be made on an as-needed or as-desired basis.

What Can We Believe?

Given the skeptic's claims, we would expect that there would be several contenders for the place of "most likely contact from a creator". In my view at least, the Bible presents a claim of contact by God with His creation that stands apart from all other candidates. I have no doubt that some will disagree and I do not expect to change their minds. They are free to perform their own search, reach their own conclusions, and live with their own results. I address believers who sincerely ask questions such as: Is this all we know? Can we not find more, especially better, evidence that the Bible is the genuine recorded contact between our creator and ourselves?

The Evaluation

Students of a security field may recognize the previous section as the process of *identification*. The God of the Bible has identified Himself as our creator. What remains is *authentication*—Is the God of the Bible really the God He claims to be or an impostor?

The problem that we are addressing is that we cannot discover, learn about, or communicate with the creator. The communication gap between creator and creation can only be bridged by the creator. Con-

The Evaluation

tinuing along those lines, we can say that the burden of validating the communication from the creator must also rest with the creator. We cannot verify the authenticity of the communication by ourselves. The creator must therefore provide proof (authentication) of his identity. We would hope that our creator would provide such proof, knowing that we would have to face scoffers and skeptics.

So, is there anything in the Bible that gives us such proof? In the light of what we discovered in Chapter 2, could there be anything that the creator could provide and that we are able to authenticate? Fortunately, we seem to be much better at checking the validity of a proof than we are at providing the proof itself. Formulating a proof is difficult and may even be impossible. Given a valid proof, formalizing that proof is an arduous but feasible task. Verifying the formal proof is easy enough that the job can be handled by a machine.

So, authentication should be possible. We are capable of understanding and validating a proof of authentication if we have one. But has God provided a proof of His communication with us?

The Bible presents prophecy as a proof of authenticity. Prophecy, in particular prophecy describing events before they take place, might work. Anyone can guess at future events. If those events come to pass, the person who made the guess is not a prophet, they are just lucky. Lottery winners would be an example. Educated guesses are a little better because they use what we know about the past and present to anticipate that some future events are more likely than others. This still is not prophecy since it does not represent actual knowledge of the future, just a partial knowledge of our present trajectory.

A person could describe a future and then cause that future to happen. This is pretty routine and we refer to it with terms such as planning, goal-setting, and working. What separates us from prophets? A prophet as I am using that term is someone who describes future events reliably. When we make plans and set goals, we don't always achieve them. We just aren't powerful enough to achieve all of them. If we limit ourselves to plans and goals that are so simple we don't think we could possibly fail, we might consider ourselves to be prophets in this limited context. But even then, circumstances can arise that interfere with our plans no matter how simple they may be. We can prophesy that the sun will rise much more reliably than we can prophesy about any action we

The Evaluation

may intend to take. The creator we are considering is sufficiently powerful that His plans are always accomplished.

A few years ago, there was much attention given to the study of what is known as *chaos theory*. In essence, that theory says that while the physical processes that underly the universe may be deterministic (disputing this only reinforces the implications of the theory), the scale of the universe and most subsets thereof is too large for us to project the future with any degree of accuracy for very long. This is exactly the problem faced in weather forecasting. Forecasters can predict weather with reasonable, although imperfect, accuracy for the immediate future. As the length of the forecast grows, the accuracy diminishes, *rapidly*. Chaos theory captures the idea that there are too many variables, most of which we are not even aware of, for us to take them into account for more than a very short duration. Provided that this theory holds, it is not possible to predict the future to produce a prophecy that is accurate, detailed, and extensive.

We might think that some "really smart" person could take enough variables into account that they could provide very accurate predictions for a longer interval. How would we tell the difference? As has been the premise of many fictional stories, knowledge of the future will invalidate that particular future. That is, if we know the future, we will behave differently than if we did not have the knowledge. The smart person would have to take that into account. But if knowledge of the future invalidates that known future, what future could such a person tell us about that would actually transpire? Only a future that we don't care enough about to change our behavior. Even the tiniest change in our behavior will have ramifications that grow quickly to become large changes in future events, possibly far removed from ourselves. That means such a person can tell us the future provided it is a future that we do not participate in and do not want to participate in. The same must be true of anyone we relayed the prediction to. It would be like knowing winning lottery numbers while marooned on an island.

Prophecy could come from factual knowledge of the future. Who could have such factual knowledge? Only someone who has observed it, perhaps someone with the ability to communicate backward in time or the ability to observe events at future times. Such a person could then communicate to us what they have observed before we observe it in the present. However, the previous argument still ap-

The Evaluation

plies. They would be observing a future and then altering the past that produced that future. The altered past yields a future that is not the same as the one that was observed. Chaos theory contends that even tiny disturbances in the present are magnified rapidly to have very large effects in the future.

Doesn't this also prevent the creator from giving us prophecy? No! The creator is not making a prediction or observation. The creator has created time and that implies not just the existence of time, but also the things that appear in time, which is to say, *history*. The creator created the dimensions of space, the matter, energy, and whatever else or whatever less that we may find there, and he created history.

Prophecy, when provided by the creator, is simply telling us what exists in the history the creator made. Our reaction to our knowledge of the prophecy has already been taken into account in that history. So, a creator is able to provide prophecy as proof of identity that cannot be forged by anyone within the created universe. It can't even be forged by someone who also exists outside of creation and is telling us what they see but did not create. To do so would alter the creation and invalidate all prophecies. If we have such a prophecy, and especially if we have many such prophecies, we know the person who provided them is the creator.

This also suggests that the creator is somewhat unique. Consider the case that there were two independent persons outside creation, one is creator and the other is not. If the non-creator makes contact with the creation, that creation is then changed. The consequence of such a tampering with the creation is that those changes invalidate all prophecies. So, either such persons are co-creators to some degree, or they never tamper with (contact) the creation.

Note that in this section, I have made reference to persons outside creation as if they, too, exist within time (e.g., when I say they never tamper with the creation). But such persons do not exist within time and terms like "never" don't really apply. I have used these terms wittingly to avoid cumbersome and pedantic alternatives.

Prophecies

That is all well and good, but do we have such prophecies? I think so.

Chapter 1 began with a prophecy recorded by the apostle Peter. The skeptic might want to challenge the interpretations that I made to show that this

Prophecies

prophecy has been fulfilled in our presence. This brings us back to the previously discussed challenge of deciding what constitutes an acceptable proof. You must decide for yourself if you consider my interpretations to be likely or not.

There are many prophecies in the Old Testament relating to the future of Israel. Some have been fulfilled and some have not. The prophecies relating to the deportation of Judah to Babylon were made long before that event happened. The exact time (70 years, Jeremiah 27:10-12, 29:10) of the return of the exiles to Jerusalem was recorded before the beginning of the exile. The name of the king of Medo-Persia (Cyrus, Isaiah 44:28) who would grant permission for the return from exile was given before Cyrus was born.

These are just a few of the prophecies that have been given and fulfilled. The skeptic has no difficulty addressing these by simply refusing to believe that this is genuine prophecy. They can say that these prophecies were obviously written after the historical events took place. There isn't much to say to that. They do call themselves skeptics for good reason.

There are prophecies throughout the Old Testament, as early as the promises made to Abraham, relating to the future of Israel that were not fulfilled. These prophecies must either be fulfilled or they discredit the prophet. If the creator tells us about the future that he has created and that future does not come to pass, he must be lying.

What about those unfulfilled prophecies about the future of Israel? Do they discredit the Bible? Perhaps we might have thought so a century ago. Israel was not a sovereign nation for most of 2,500 years. Even worse, the Israelites themselves were scattered across the globe. Without a nation of Israel, those prophecies would seem to provide proof that the Bible was not the authentic word of God.

In all of recorded history, no people group has ever been defeated/disbursed/disbanded for such a long period of time and maintained their identity. Yet the Israelites have maintained their identity in the places to which they have been dispersed. There was a growing and very productive movement in the 20th century to regather them to the former land of Israel. That process was so successful that they received worldwide recognition as a sovereign nation in 1948. This is the most sovereignty the nation of Israel has had in almost 2,500 years. That is an unprecedented event.

Prophecies

It is also a prophetic event. Before 1948, there were those who recognized that the reestablishment of the nation of Israel must eventually happen. They didn't have a date for the event, but they did have a need (prophecies related to the nation that were not yet fulfilled) as well as explicit prophecies such as that of Ezekiel 37.

We can't say that Ezekiel's prophecy is a forgery that was written after 1948. International recognition of Israel's sovereignty might have been influenced by the prophecy. Recognition was the product of Jewish advocacy. Were they aware of Ezekiel's prophecy? I'm sure they were, but that only provides the mechanism for the fulfillment of prophecy. The validity of the prophecy is not diminished.

Some might believe that this was just coincidence. I don't think so. The specificity of Ezekiel's prophecy combined with 2,500 years in which Israel was ruled by other nations, occupied by other races, and dispersed throughout the world make this a coincidence of extreme improbability. Here we have a prophecy that has been fulfilled too recently for the historical accuracy of the event to be dismissed. It also paves the way for fulfillment of many other prophecies relating to Israel as a people, a sovereign nation, and a kingdom.

What Can We Believe?

Prophecy is a resource only available to believers—scoffers have nothing comparable. Ultimately, each person must decide for themselves what they are going to believe. You can just follow what other people believe, but I don't recommend that. You really should look into the available information and decide for yourself. The best skeptics make quite an effort to do this. They spend a lot of time looking at the various alternatives and deciding not to believe that God, as presented in the Bible, is literally real. My purpose here is not to change their beliefs. It is to show the reader what he must disbelieve if he is going to be a skeptic.

4. Perilous Times

This know also, that in the last days perilous times shall come. For men shall be lovers of their own selves, covetous, boasters, proud, blasphemers, disobedient to parents, unthankful, unholy, Without natural affection, trucebreakers, false accusers, incontinent, fierce, despisers of those that are good, Traitors, heady, highminded, lovers of pleasures more than lovers of God; Having a form of godliness, but denying the power thereof: from such turn away. For of this sort are they which creep into houses, and lead captive silly women laden with sins, led away with divers lusts, Ever learning, and never able to come to the knowledge of the truth.
II Timothy 3:1–7, KJV

Peter tells us about scoffers who would dispute the return of the Christ. He describes scoffers, but does not tell us what will become of them. Perhaps they are rebuffed? Maybe one of the reasons that prophecy is given is to equip Christians with the information they need to stop scoffers? On the other hand, maybe scoffers are successful in their campaign against the cause of Christ. Does our notably Christian culture die at the hands of scoffers?

Having a Form of Godliness

Here the apostle Paul describes a period of the last days in which people and culture are in a pitifully poor state. We might identify this description with many cultures and peoples, but Paul says these will come in the last days. In some way, these people will be uniquely identifiable as a group. So, who are these people? At first, we might react to these verses by thinking that they are a description of those who do not acknowledge God. I think a closer inspection suggests otherwise.

First, we notice they have a form of godliness. That doesn't fit a people who reject the very idea of a creator. The phrase "ever learning" brings to mind a developed system of education such as exists today throughout much of the world; but in the pursuit of this education, they are not able to acquire the knowledge of the truth. This is suggesting that they are trying to come to the knowledge of the truth. They are also lovers of pleasure *more* than they are lovers of God. That suggests that they don't profess to hate God, but that they love pleasure more. To me at least, these phrases indicate that the people we are looking at here are the remnants of an apostate church. They have a form of godliness, but deny the power, and from these we are instructed to turn away. That would indicate that they claim to be Christian, but do not hold the gospel of Jesus Christ. If they were merely unbelievers, we would be instructed to be a witness to them, but not to adopt their standards and behavior, which often differ from God's standards and behaviors. The apostate and the false teachers we are to avoid, they deceive and corrupt the church from the inside.

So aside from being an apostate church, who are these people? I suggest that these may be the product of scoffers. People who were persuaded that what God wrote about creation and judgment was not true and, therefore, the second coming is also not true. From there they have turned away from the rest of what God wrote. I find it difficult to explain why some people who do not believe in the truth of the Word of God, the literalness of God, and the power of the creator, want to associate with the church. As Paul said, if there is no resurrection, we of all people are most pitiful (I Corinthians 15:16-19). Being a Christian only makes sense if what God has written is true. All of it. These people want to say they are Christian and possibly go to church regularly and probably do good works, but why? If God is as impotent as they apparently believe He is, why bother? Paul doesn't provide an explanation here.

Lovers of Their Own Selves

These people will love themselves. It is common at this time to hear people say that you should love yourself, and whether we say it or not, it is not an unusual attitude for us to have. God instructs us to love our neighbor as we love ourselves (or as much as we love ourselves) and also tells us that no man ever yet hated his own body (Matthew 19:19, Ephesians 5:29). So this criticism isn't about people who care about their own wellbeing, that is not condemned anywhere. In the context of Paul's prophecy, we can see that these people love themselves to the extent that they do not (or no longer) practice loving their neighbor.

In the perilous times, the advice to love yourself will be practiced by a people who profess to be Christian, and that directly contradicts God's instruction that we should love our neighbor. It is easy to see that a people who emphasize a love of themselves and cease to love their neighbor would fall into the long list of sins found here, sins against their neighbors and sins against God.

Despisers of Those That Are Good

> *When ye say, Every one that doeth evil is good in the sight of the Lord, and he delighteth in them ...*
> Malachi 2:17b

There is a sense in which it is counter intuitive that people who choose to be sinful will also hate people who choose not to be. But we have to remember that when people sin, they do not like to be reminded of their sin. None of us do. But when we are reminded, we all have a choice. We can acknowledge the sin to God and put it behind us with the intention of not continuing in sin, or we can refuse to do so. The people Paul is describing have faced the fact that they are practicing sin and have chosen to continue. They are *lovers of pleasures more than lovers of God.*

The words of the prophet Malachi that are quoted above were some of the last words recorded for Israel in the Old Testament, and they are spoken against the priests of Israel. The priests, the spiritual leaders, were telling the Israelites that those who did evil were actually doing good and that God approved.

I have witnessed a false teacher who did this very thing. About the normalization of a behavior God has clearly labeled to be sin, he said it was good and that God approved. I think one of the attributes that we can use to identify the last days is that leaders in the church will be guilty of the sin of labeling evil as good and saying that God approves of the evil conduct. With leadership such as this, Christians must become familiar with the things God has written for us so that we can know when we are being lied to by a false teacher. These are perilous times.

In the last days, apostate Christians will despise those who do not join them in their apostasy. They want to be told that the things they do are good and that God approves. When they see someone who does differently, they will be offended and they will despise those who do what is right. This may be the cause for making false accusations and other sins against those who are saved.

The Days of Noah

But as the days of Noah were, so shall also the coming of the Son of man be. For as in the days that were before the flood they were eating and drinking, marrying and giving in marriage, until the day that Noe entered into the ark,

The Days of Noah

And knew not until the flood came, and took them all away; so shall also the coming of the Son of man be.
Matthew 24:37-39

The period of last days that we have been considering is the last days prior to the second coming of Jesus. Scoffers begin by showing that it won't happen and end with the surprise of seeing it happen with their own eyes. This period is characterized by being similar to the days of Noah. The apostle Peter characterized Noah as a preacher of righteousness (II Peter 2:5). Noah told the inhabitants of the earth that judgment was coming and apparently, they dismissed his words. They carried on as if their behavior would have no consequences. What characterized those days?

And God saw that the wickedness of man was great in the earth, and that every imagination of the thoughts of his heart was only evil continually. And it repented the Lord that he had made man on the earth, and it grieved him at his heart. And the Lord said, I will destroy man whom I have created from the face of the earth; both man, and beast, and the creeping thing, and the fowls of the air; for it repenteth me that I have made them.

The earth also was corrupt before God, and the earth was filled with violence. And God looked upon the earth, and,

Perilous Times

behold, it was corrupt; for all flesh had corrupted his way upon the earth.
Genesis 6:5-7, 6:11-12

The popular modern standard of human depravity is usually found in the atrocities of Nazi Germany during the 1930s and 1940s. Whether these atrocities compare to the violence and corruption of Noah's day, we can't really say. But most of the remainder of the world was appalled by what they eventually saw in Germany. So, the corruption, however severe it may have been in comparison, was not global.

The days of Noah were marked by almost total decay and on a global scale. Violence and the corruption of their behavior was such that it was time for God to put a stop to it. God hasn't put a stop to violence or corruption like this since Noah's day. That tells us that the human race had deteriorated beyond anything that has been seen since. That is what we can expect from the last days before the second coming. When the apostle Paul wrote that the last days would be perilous times, this is what that means. It is violent and corrupt in the extreme.

What Should We Do?

> *And he saith unto me, Seal not the sayings of the prophecy of this book: for the time is at hand. He that is unjust, let him be unjust still: and he which is filthy, let him be filthy still: and he that is righteous, let him be righteous still: and he that is holy, let him be holy still. And, behold, I come quickly; and my reward is with me, to give every man according as his work shall be.*
> Revelation 22:10-11

The second coming is the next big item on God's agenda. When He comes, He will have His reward with Him. Those who are unjust will continue to be unjust and receive the reward of the unjust. Those who are holy will continue to be holy and receive the reward of the holy.

The book of Revelation records seven letters that were written to seven churches. Those letters provide instruction for the environment and condition each church was in. We, too, can use these instructions for a guide to ourselves for any environment and condition in which we find ourselves.

Perilous Times

Unto the angel of the church of Ephesus write;

These things saith he that holdeth the seven stars in his right hand, who walketh in the midst of the seven golden candlesticks; I know thy works, and thy labour, and thy patience, and how thou canst not bear them which are evil: and thou hast tried them which say they are apostles, and are not, and hast found them liars: And hast borne, and hast patience, and for my name's sake hast laboured, and hast not fainted. Nevertheless I have somewhat against thee, because thou hast left thy first love. Remember therefore from whence thou art fallen, and repent, and do the first works; or else I will come unto thee quickly, and will remove thy candlestick out of his place, except thou repent. But this thou hast, that thou hatest the deeds of the Nicolaitanes, which I also hate.

He that hath an ear, let him hear what the Spirit saith unto the churches; To him that overcometh will I give to eat of the tree of life, which is in the midst of the paradise of God.
Revelation 22:10-12

The church at Ephesus started well. They found evil people to be unbearable and were able to see through false apostles. However, they had lost their devotion to Jesus. Jesus reminds them to return to their earlier good works so that they might receive the reward that was within their reach. When we apply these admonitions in our own lives, we should not be so super-

What Should We Do?

ficial as to think that just any "good works" will do. The earlier good works of the Ephesians were works of faithfulness to things they were taught by the apostle Paul and other disciples.

> *And unto the angel of the church in Smyrna write;*
>
> *These things saith the first and the last, which was dead, and is alive; I know thy works, and tribulation, and poverty, (but thou art rich) and I know the blasphemy of them which say they are Jews, and are not, but are the synagogue of Satan. Fear none of those things which thou shalt suffer: behold, the devil shall cast some of you into prison, that ye may be tried; and ye shall have tribulation ten days: be thou faithful unto death, and I will give thee a crown of life.*
>
> *He that hath an ear, let him hear what the Spirit saith unto the churches; He that overcometh shall not be hurt of the second death.*
> Revelation 2:8-11

The church at Smyrna was faithful through poverty and hardship. They would be persecuted even more, and God reminds them that their difficulties were not permanent. His reward is greater and more secure than anything they might have on the earth, including the reward of eternal life. We should not forget that important truth either. We are also reminded here, and we probably need to be reminded, that it is ultimately Satan who persecutes Christians for their faithfulness.

> *And to the angel of the church in Pergamos write;*
>
> *These things saith he which hath the sharp sword with two edges; I know thy works, and where thou dwellest, even where Satan's seat is: and thou holdest fast my name, and hast not denied my faith, even in those days wherein Antipas was my faithful martyr, who was slain among you, where Satan dwelleth. But I have a few things against thee, because thou hast there them that hold the doctrine of Balaam, who taught Balac to cast a stumblingblock before the children of Israel, to eat things sacrificed unto idols, and to commit fornication. So hast thou also them that hold the doctrine of the Nicolaitanes, which thing I hate. Repent; or else I will come unto thee quickly, and will fight against them with the sword of my mouth.*
>
> *He that hath an ear, let him hear what the Spirit saith unto the churches; To him that overcometh will I give to eat of the hidden manna, and will give him a white stone, and in the stone a new name written, which no man knoweth saving he that receiveth it.*
> Revelation 2:12-17

The church at Pergamos included some who taught things contrary to God's teaching, things that God

What Should We Do?

had declared to be immoral and sinful. Balaam had carried out a campaign of temptation to do damage to Israel. This church was suffering harm from a similar tactic employed to introduce the false teaching of the Nicolaitans, which did not regard explicitly sinful behavior as something to be avoided.

God carries a double-edged sword and they were instructed to stop practicing those things or God Himself would put a stop to it. All Christians do well to pay attention to the things we tolerate and justify. If we are justifying things that God has identified as sin and we do not make the necessary corrections, the time will come when God makes those corrections Himself.

> *And unto the angel of the church in Thyatira write;*
>
> *These things saith the Son of God, who hath his eyes like unto a flame of fire, and his feet are like fine brass; I know thy works, and charity, and service, and faith, and thy patience, and thy works; and the last to be more than the first. Notwithstanding I have a few things against thee, because thou sufferest that woman Jezebel, which calleth herself a prophetess, to teach and to seduce my servants to commit fornication, and to eat things sacrificed unto idols. And I gave her space to repent of her fornication; and she repented not. Behold, I will cast her into a bed, and them that commit adultery with her into*

great tribulation, except they repent of their deeds. And I will kill her children with death; and all the churches shall know that I am he which searcheth the reins and hearts: and I will give unto every one of you according to your works.

But unto you I say, and unto the rest in Thyatira, as many as have not this doctrine, and which have not known the depths of Satan, as they speak; I will put upon you none other burden. But that which ye have already hold fast till I come. And he that overcometh, and keepeth my works unto the end, to him will I give power over the nations:

And he shall rule them with a rod of iron; as the vessels of a potter shall they be broken to shivers: even as I received of my Father. And I will give him the morning star.

He that hath an ear, let him hear what the Spirit saith unto the churches.
Revelation 2:19-29

The good works of the church in Thyatira had grown greater since the time that church began. However, they had a very specific fault of tolerating a woman who falsely claimed to be a prophetess, which she used as a platform to seduce members of the church. God told them that those who failed to turn away from this sin would be made an example to the other churches. Those who had not fallen into her trap

What Should We Do?

God instructs to continue in their good works until He comes.

This Jezebel was not just sinning herself; she was seducing others in the church to sin. Corrupting the church in this way made dealing with this problem in the church all the more important. Even so, God gave her time to repent. She would be an example of the seriousness of this open and rebellious sin. She could provide the example through repentance or God would make an example of her.

> *And unto the angel of the church in Sardis write;*
>
> *These things saith he that hath the seven Spirits of God, and the seven stars; I know thy works, that thou hast a name that thou livest, and art dead. Be watchful, and strengthen the things which remain, that are ready to die: for I have not found thy works perfect before God. Remember therefore how thou hast received and heard, and hold fast, and repent. If therefore thou shalt not watch, I will come on thee as a thief, and thou shalt not know what hour I will come upon thee. Thou hast a few names even in Sardis which have not defiled their garments; and they shall walk with me in white: for they are worthy. He that overcometh, the same shall be clothed in white raiment; and I will not blot out his name out of the book of life, but I will confess his name before my Father, and before his angels.*

Perilous Times

He that hath an ear, let him hear what the Spirit saith unto the churches.
Revelation 3:1-6

The church at Sardis had the outward appearance of being vibrant and alive, but in God's eyes, it was actually dead. They are instructed to find and nourish those parts that are not yet dead and to remember the things they had been taught when they began. If they failed, they would be caught by surprise by Jesus' return and only the few that had remained faithful to the things the church once believed would find their names in the Book of Life.

This letter plainly indicates that a Christian may find themselves in a church composed mainly of people whose faith is essentially dead. This letter doesn't say those Christians must leave, probably because the faithful Christian continues to be a witness to the rest of the church. Such Christian's rewards are secure because they will be given for individual faithfulness, not the faithfulness of their church.

And to the angel of the church in Philadelphia write;

These things saith he that is holy, he that is true, he that hath the key of David, he that openeth, and no man shutteth; and shutteth, and no man openeth; I know thy works: behold, I have set before thee an open door, and

What Should We Do?

no man can shut it: for thou hast a little strength, and hast kept my word, and hast not denied my name. Behold, I will make them of the synagogue of Satan, which say they are Jews, and are not, but do lie; behold, I will make them to come and worship before thy feet, and to know that I have loved thee. Because thou hast kept the word of my patience, I also will keep thee from the hour of temptation, which shall come upon all the world, to try them that dwell upon the earth. Behold, I come quickly: hold that fast which thou hast, that no man take thy crown. Him that overcometh will I make a pillar in the temple of my God, and he shall go no more out: and I will write upon him the name of my God, and the name of the city of my God, which is new Jerusalem, which cometh down out of heaven from my God: and I will write upon him my new name.

He that hath an ear, let him hear what the Spirit saith unto the churches.
Revelation 3:7-13

The church at Philadelphia was not strong materially, but it had persevered in faithfulness. God did not need to give words of correction to this church, just encouragement to continue in faithfulness and a preview of the rewards that God had for them.

The members of this church were despised by Jews who God said were not genuine, that is, not faithful. Another encouragement to this church is that those people would someday see God show His love for this church and they would be despised no more.

One of the rewards listed here is that they would be spared a trial that God would be bringing upon the whole world. This is interesting because it is a reward for faithfulness that is given to them while they are still here on the earth. Most of the other rewards that are mentioned are received in heaven.

> *And unto the angel of the church of the Laodiceans write;*
>
> *These things saith the Amen, the faithful and true witness, the beginning of the creation of God; I know thy works, that thou art neither cold nor hot: I would thou wert cold or hot. So then because thou art lukewarm, and neither cold nor hot, I will spue thee out of my mouth. Because thou sayest, I am rich, and increased with goods, and have need of nothing; and knowest not that thou art wretched, and miserable, and poor, and blind, and naked: I counsel thee to buy of me gold tried in the fire, that thou mayest be rich; and white raiment, that thou mayest be clothed, and that the shame of thy nakedness do not appear; and anoint thine eyes with eyesalve, that thou mayest see. As many as I love, I rebuke and chasten: be zealous therefore, and repent. Behold, I stand at the door, and knock: if any man hear my voice, and open the door, I will come in to him, and will sup with him, and*

What Should We Do?

he with me. To him that overcometh will I grant to sit with me in my throne, even as I also overcame, and am set down with my Father in his throne.

He that hath an ear, let him hear what the Spirit saith unto the churches.

Revelation 3:14-22

The church of the Laodiceans was not especially sinful, but not righteous either. It was prosperous but not spiritually. God says He finds this especially distasteful. If they were righteous, He would love and reward them. If they were evil, He would hate and condemn them. Since they are neither, they make God sick.

Their instruction amounts to, "Stop playing Christian and get serious." If they respond to God's knock, He will teach them to be prosperous spiritually and they will be welcome at the throne of God. If they don't, they are refused admittance. Anyone who doesn't answer His knock may not be as actively sinful as the evil people called out in other churches, but they are sinful. By failing to answer, they do not receive forgiveness and remain condemned, although perhaps with less vengeance. Perhaps the lesson here can be summarized by saying that prosperity does not imply approval.

I think it is particularly important for us to notice how many of the problems encountered by these churches were related to people in positions of authority who were teaching sinful practices and deceiving church members. In each case, the church is told that they had been taught the truth and thus had no excuse for being deceived. The instructions to the seven churches are given for the purpose of securing the rewards that Jesus will bring with Him at His second coming. We do well to pay attention to these instructions and apply them ourselves as needed.

Knowledge

> *Now as touching things offered unto idols, we know that we all have knowledge. Knowledge puffeth up, but charity edifieth. And if any man think that he knoweth any thing, he knoweth nothing yet as he ought to know.*
> I Corinthians 8:1-2

So, what shall we do with knowledge? We live in a culture that is obsessed with knowledge. The apostle Paul says we all have knowledge, but when we dwell on the knowledge, we have we are puffed up, arrogant. We fail to recognize that no matter how much knowledge we acquire, we continue to know so little that it isn't really significant. I think most of us would

Knowledge

agree that arrogance benefits no one. Conversely, love edifies, that is, love benefits those around us. Knowledge is elusive, but love is freely available.

> *And though I have the gift of prophecy, and understand all mysteries, and all knowledge; and though I have all faith, so that I could remove mountains, and have not charity* (love), *I am nothing. And though I bestow all my goods to feed the poor, and though I give my body to be burned, and have not charity, it profiteth me nothing.*
>
> *Charity suffereth long, and is kind; charity envieth not; charity vaunteth not itself, is not puffed up, Doth not behave itself unseemly, seeketh not her own, is not easily provoked, thinketh no evil; Rejoiceth not in iniquity, but rejoiceth in the truth; Beareth all things, believeth all things, hopeth all things, endureth all things.*
>
> *Charity never faileth: but whether there be prophecies, they shall fail; whether there be tongues, they shall cease; whether there be knowledge, it shall vanish away.*
> I Corinthians 13:2-8

The apostle is emphasizing that love, as God recognizes love, is most important. Everything else can and will fail us, but it is love and love alone that endures. He is not saying that the other things, such as knowledge and good works, are not worthwhile. He is saying that without love, they are without value. In the last days, knowledge will increase and men will be ever-learning, but their love will be for themselves because they are puffed up by such knowledge as they are able to acquire.

Summary

I do not think we have yet reached the stage of the last days of the church period described by Paul, or at least not to the full extent. We may, however, be seeing the beginnings of the things Paul warned about. We do well to watch the events that unfold around us while being mindful that the days described by Paul may appear soon.

5. Christians

We have examined what the scoffers have to say, and other critics of Christianity say similar things. They have proposed the axiom of uniformitarianism and from this they say that it follows that the earth is very old. Extending these ideas, they have concluded that life evolved on the earth over long periods of time in contrast to what is recorded in the Bible. Next, they make a very great leap and conclude that life appeared spontaneously and that no creator was involved. Finally, the greatest claim of all is that evidence makes these conclusions inescapable.

What are Christians supposed to think? A variety of positions have been taken under the umbrella of Christianity. Among those taking such positions, some are genuine born-again believers in Christ and some are not. The position I have presented in this book is that the description of creation presented in the book of Genesis is historically accurate to the extent that the universe was created over a period of six days of ordinary length. Obviously, no natural process could be responsible for that. But then, no natural process could be responsible for the existence of a universe at all.

Present-day Christians taking the "young earth" position generally agree on the importance and the value that science provides. The disagreement with scoffers begins with a difference of axioms. The scoffer begins with an assumption of non-creation and the Christian assumes that we are created. Human reason will find support and draw conclusions that align with these initial assumptions. That is why no real belief system exists without a religious component. The scoffer is religious too, even if they are trying not to be. They have faith and a lot of zeal in defending that faith from opposing views.

From a platform of religion-free science we can't expect to make progress toward anything. There must be faith in something to give the scientist some direction. Uniformitarianism and atheism have directed the scoffer to the conclusion that science proves the earth to be very old and there is no creator. Obviously, this can be proven true; these are his axioms! Similarly, the Christian starts with a belief in the creator described in Genesis and concludes that we were created and the earth is not so old as the scoffer says. Postmodern philosophy draws on the collected knowledge of all of humanity to show that neither position can be more valid than the other.

I have made the claim that the post-modernist is correct insofar as human reason is able to ascertain. But I further claim that the Christian has access to more information than a naturalist or humanist has. A creator need not be subject to the constraints that we humans must live with. He can tell us what we are unable to prove for ourselves. The value in this is twofold. The creators' information can overcome our bias to direct us toward his truth, and the creators' information can also provide a confirmation of truth that we are unable to obtain ourselves. It is this additional information, and only this additional information, that repudiates the conclusions of postmodern philosophy.

We are able to reason because we were created to do so. The universe conforms to an orderly set of rules that can be studied by scientists because God created the universe to be orderly. We and the universe fail to live up to these created purposes when separated from God and that separation began when Adam sinned. Scoffers suffer from willful bias and the universe suffers deterioration. God has explained all of this in advance and we have observed it happening.

Christians

It can still be difficult to come to terms with the idea that millions of scientists can suffer the same bias at the same time and reach the same erroneous conclusions. God provides us with additional information here as well. Scoffers do not take into account the adversary, the first to rebel against his creator. This adversary has determined to do as much damage to God's creation as possible, although his motivation is not entirely clear to me. Apparently, he knows he will eventually be defeated at an appointed time, but still he continues doing what damage he can.

God calls this adversary the great deceiver (Revelation 12:9), able to deceive the whole world with the exception of those whose faith is in God. We know that faith is fundamental to knowledge, and a faith in legitimate truth is resistant to deception. Scientists who do not have a faith in the truth God has provided can be manipulated by the adversary to serve the goals of the adversary, which is to do as much damage to God's creation as possible. The physical creation is a low priority target for this adversary, his focus is on the human race. God tells Christians they are His heirs (Romans 8:16-17). We are a rich target for someone God describes as a "murderer from the beginning" and a deceiver "because there is no truth in him" (John 8:44).

The world we live in makes sense. It makes sense because it was created and our creator has explained it to us. We are imbued with the capacity to understand His communication and relate it to what we see around us. The value of a good educational system is that it can greatly extend this understanding by bringing to our attention information from many sources including theology, history, and science.

Many people now believe that what God has said does not harmonize with what we observe. Certainly, that is true for our critics. What God has said does not agree with what the critics believe. However, that is not the same as saying that what God has said *cannot* agree with what we observe. We can look for harmony between God's Word and man's knowledge. Many have engaged in just that effort and reached many conclusions. Some of these conclusions have produced theories that attempt to harmonize the Word of God with science. Implicitly, this assumes that science is the more reliable knowledge. As I have attempted to show, science is not immutable. In fact, the process of revision is an integral part of science. That is what is meant by scientific progress—finding errors and omissions in scientific knowledge and making improvements. In contrast, the Word of God is monotonic, meaning that as new knowledge was added existing knowledge was preserved. Over a period of many generations, God added to His written record without nullifying what was already recorded.

Hopefully, by this time you realize that there are many ways to approach the task of relating what God has said and what we observe. And you should recognize that they do not yield the same results or even correct results. The mutability of science makes the "science first" approach of dubious value and it doesn't even stand up to reason. If the Word of God is provided by God, how could it be wrong? If you accept that reasoning, you should also be able to see that we can approach this task "scripture first." Here we search for scientifically valid and sound theories that explain our observations without violating what God has written. If the Word of God is genuine, we should reasonably expect to find these theories. Such theories are a product of human reason and therefore subject to human error. But they do have the benefit of beginning with axioms that are not of fragile human origin.

Our critics say that such theories do not exist. We are free to take their word for that, but the consequences of being wrong are severe. We are pretty poor excuse for "intelligent beings" if we don't even bother to verify such important claims that are being given to us. We are most fortunate to have highly qualified people that do look into the veracity of these claims. They have told us (see Chapter 6) what they have found. Theories that are both scientifically valid and consistent with God's written Word have been proposed, and problems with the critic's own theories abound. We have no excuse for ignorance, we can evaluate for ourselves the claims of the critic and the claims of the Christian.

Our critics sometimes object to creation, saying that without evolution, science will be irreparably harmed, or that evolution is essential to the advancement of science. Modern science is a product of western culture and it has thrived here even though it has been a Christian culture as well. The success and productivity of science is positively correlated with culture's Christian content. There seems to be no basis for this objection by the critic.

There are scientists who are Christian that counter this objection with the counter claim that science is harmed by the theory of evolution. This objection seems valid to me. Conclusive evidence for evolution has been so difficult to find that it is no longer expected or required. Scholarly publications can be found that assert that some phenomenon being studied is the product of evolution. They provide no justification for their assertion—it is just accepted. This is not the norm for scholarly publications. Scholars are usually required to justify any and every assertion, either within the publication or by reference. The requirements for publication are policed by the peer review process. But the peers suffer from the same lack of evidence as authors so it is to everyone's advantage to accept these assertions as is. In effect, evolution is no longer a theory. It has quietly become an axiom, and thus exempt from the demand for proof.

Christian authors, some with works listed in Chapter 6, have written that science was not highly successful until it was embraced by Christian culture. They contend that to have the level of success that we have had, scientists needed a reason to think that the universe is constructed conforming to a consistent set of rules. Without such a set of rules, there is nothing for the scientist to study. Early science in pagan cultures was derailed by the lack of this basic assumption.

Today, non-Christians abound in science, so what reason do they have for thinking that the universe has a structure that can be studied? Obviously, the success of previous generations of scientists is a good reason. But without a creator, what reason can they give for that? I don't know of a reason other than "just because." The modern non-Christian knows the universe conforms to a set of rules but doesn't know why. Ironically, they do know the one rule that confounds them:

Creation denies them access to absolute truth.

6. Suggested Reading

An important topic that I have discussed in this book has been the scoffers—who they are, what they are doing, and what to think about their claims. The fundamental issue scoffers use to give themselves credibility is the issue of origins. God says He created the universe in six days and scoffers say He had nothing to do with it. We are all more or less familiar with the evidence scoffers provide for what they believe. Here I want to provide a list of sources that offers an alternative interpretation of the evidence. These sources show an interpretation of scientific evidence that strongly supports the biblical account.

The Genesis Flood
John C. Whitcomb and Henry M. Morris
P&R Publishing
ISBN 978-1-59638-395-1

This is a landmark book in the effort to stand up to scoffers. It is credited with revitalizing the belief in

Suggested Reading

biblical inerrancy on the subject of creation and the flood. It is a good place to start learning about the history of the debate surrounding creation and evolution and why the flood and a young earth continue to be scientifically reasonable theories.

The Evolution Handbook
Vance Ferrell
Evolution Facts, Inc.
Box 300
Altamont, TN 37301
931-692-5777
evolution-facts.org

This rather long book is not a primary source for the information it provides. It is a collection of facts and quotations addressing all areas of the creation-evolution debate. This book is an excellent resource for quickly obtaining a broad understanding of the issues that have been raised with respect to evolution and the history of evolutionary and creationist research.

Genetic Entropy and the Mystery of the Genome
Dr. J.C. Sanford
Third Edition
ISBN 978-0-9816316-0-8
FMS Publications

There are two very fundamental and very necessary elements of the theory of evolution. First, there must be genetic mutation. Mutations produce new and varied forms of life from the life that already exists, and only genetic mutation can be passed on to subsequent generations of life. Second, natural selection must "prune" counterproductive mutations while retaining those that are beneficial.

In this book, Dr. Sanford mathematically examines the plausibility of these elements. He shows that the corrective influence of natural selection is grossly overwhelmed by the pace of mutation. That means that harmful mutations are accumulating much faster than natural selection can remove them. The problem is so extreme that the entire history of human life may not last for more than a few tens of thousands of years at its current pace of deterioration. All life, including human life, is dying by the very mechanisms that are supposed to be improving it.

Suggested Reading

A most powerful feature of this work is that Dr. Sanford's analysis is consistently conservative, meaning that it is deliberately biased against the conclusions that it reaches. If a theory can be shown to be unsustainable under the most favorable of conditions, the validity of the theory is truly suspect.

I have already written about how God uses geology as the principal venue to expose the error of scoffers. Among those books outside of geology, this book provides the most powerful evidence that scoffers are promoting an illusion.

Darwin's Black Box
Michael J. Behe
ISBN 0-684-82754-9
0-684-83493-6
Simon & Schuster

This book is a landmark in the use of biochemistry to show that there are serious problems with theory of evolution. Dr. Behe shows that the processes at work within cells are far more complex than Darwin assumed. The problems surface when we look for an evolutionary path that is able to produce some of these cells. When several evolutionary steps must be completed before any of the steps can be considered beneficial, the result is what the author calls irreducible complexity.

The principle here is that the probability of a beneficial evolutionary development is very low. If we need two evolutionary developments that are only beneficial when they appear together, the probability of both evolving together is remote in the extreme. Since natural selection does not actively preserve non-beneficial mutations, the possibility of two developments happening consecutively does not increase the overall probability of occurrence to an appreciable degree. If three such developments are required, probabilities become impossibly small and timescales grow excessive.

Perhaps one is willing to admit one such evolutionary advance, or a few, but the author provides many examples of evolutionary developments that display irreducible complexity.

Suggested Reading

Refuting Evolution
Jonathan Sarfati
4th Edition
ISBN 978-0-949906-73-1
Creation Ministries International

This book addresses a wide array of issues in creation-evolution debate, providing more detail over fewer topics than The Evolution Handbook.

By Design
Jonathan Sarfati
ISBN: 978-0-94990672-4
Creation Ministries International

This book is much broader in its coverage than Refuting Evolution. It includes information on the history and personalities that have contributed to the discussion and provides some philosophical context.

The Genesis Account
Jonathan Sarfati
2nd Edition
ISBN 978-1-921643-91-0
Creation Ministries International

The subtitle of this book succinctly describes it as "A theological, historical and scientific commentary on Genesis 1-11". More pragmatically, I would describe it as an exhaustive treatise of the first verses of Genesis emphasizing it's on-going plausibility as a literal historical record and its importance as an integral part of the Christian worldview. The author skillfully incorporates theology, history, and science into a cohesive defense of christian faith.

About the Author

Robert Watson is a professional engineer, computer scientist, and a software and electrical design consultant. For more than 10 years he has also been a college and university professor teaching computer science and physics. He was raised in a rural environment where he continues to produce beef cattle today. Here he has had opportunity to relate the science he learned to the natural environment around him and find that sometimes they agree and sometimes they don't. Living in this environment has contributed to the journey that led to the writing of this book.

www.ingramcontent.com/pod-product-compliance
Lightning Source LLC
Chambersburg PA
CBHW072055110526
44590CB00018B/3187